WOND OF FAITH

Bishop Maxim Vasiljević

WONDER AS THE BEGINNING OF FAITH

Foreword by
Christos Yannaras

Translated by
Teodora Gita Simić

HOLY CROSS
ORTHODOX PRESS

Brookline, Massachusetts
2022

Published by
Holy Cross Orthodox Press
50 Goddard Avenue
Brookline, Massachusetts 02445

On the cover: *Ostrog Monastery*,
acrylic on canvas, 2021, Bishop Maxim

Library of Congress Cataloging-in-Publication Data

Names:	Vasiljević, Maksim, 1968- author. | Giannaras, Chrēstos, 1935- writer of foreword. | Simic, Teodora Gita, translator.
Title:	Wonder as the beginning of faith / Bishop Maxim Vasiljevic; foreword by Christos Yannaras ; translated by Teodora Gita Simić.
Description:	Brookline, Massachusetts : Holy Cross Orthodox Press, 2022. | Includes bibliographical references.
Identifiers:	ISBN: 978-1-935317-74-6 | LCCN: 2022019581
Subjects:	LCSH: Orthodox Eastern Church--Doctrines. | Spirituality. | Christian philosophy. | Philosophy, Ancient. | Philosophy, Modern. | Wonder--Religious aspects--Orthodox Eastern Church. | Faith (Christianity)--Orthodox Eastern Church. | Surprise--Religious aspects-- Orthodox Eastern Church. | Aesthetics--Religious aspects--Orthodox Eastern Church. | Grace (Theology)--Orthodox Eastern Church. | Will-- Religious aspects--Orthodox Eastern Church. | Technological innovations--Religious aspects--Orthodox Eastern Church. | Paradigms (Social sciences)--Religious aspects-- Orthodox Eastern Church.
Classification:	LCC: BX320.3 .V37 2022 | DDC: 230/.19--dc23

CONTENTS

FOREWORD
by Christos Yannaras

The author of this book, Maxim Vasiljevic, the most beloved bishop of Los Angeles, manages in this book a special (dare I say: *ecclesial*) type of writing: He does not write to teach or to make known opinions, views, acquired information, or wise conclusions from the study of wise texts bequeathed to us by the Fathers of the Church. In short, he does not write to incite or facilitate the *understanding* of ecclesial truth or teaching. He is not interested in informing the reader. The aim and purpose of the writing here is to build a *relationship* of communion with the reader, to invite him to touch the empirical truth of the Church, and to make him a participant in these empirical touches.

I would dare to say that the "logic" of this book is to transmit experience and not just understanding—that is, to work with the dynamics of poetry, not with the logic of the presentation of ideas. For example, the poet Odysseas Elytis writes: "What I know not glows within me. And yet it glows." I would say that this phrase is the clearest possible formulation of empirical and not just intellectual knowledge.

This book of Bishop Maxim ravishes and captivates, not because it "informs" us about the genesis of the ecclesial faith, but because it "leads us by the hand" to this faith, in the way that the language of art transmits the immediacy of experience.

INTRODUCTION

In recent times, I have written a series of essays presenting appraisals of certain events on the domestic and world stage. Quite spontaneously, there was an unexpected intertwining of the themes of my theological and pastoral work with the themes imposed by everyday life. The fire that engulfed Notre Dame Cathedral in Paris gave me a reason to think and write about the unconsumed faith that built classical buildings and humanity's need for it today. The encounter with Chinese culture gave me a new perspective on the topic of wonder, but also on the gaze as an aesthetic organ of knowledge.

Bypassing formal discourse, in the manner of amateurs, was so natural to me in 2019, in which the frequent invocation of "canonicity" and "orthodoxism" finally proved to be a mere mask for some. This freedom gave me an amazing speed of moving through themes and ideas of an aesthetic character. For example, "Seeing the Invisible" is a text inspired by the flourishing of life and the rhapsody of colors on the ocean floor, which illuminated the theme of the sanctity of the present moment, while the text "The White Color of a Painting Canvas" led to reflections on repentance as a movement not towards the past but towards future purity.

The life I have spent so far studying the writings of the Church Fathers has not prevented encounters with current, fateful problems that have proven to be no less complex and exciting than the ancient ones. This, among other things, is shown in the essay "Martyria as Freedom," in which I write against the camouflage and insensitivity of current representatives of political and ecclesial institutions. Changes on the global level have been a stimulus for reflections on hegemons, the political problems of migrants and modern nomads, and existential topics such as overcoming the ego and understanding the issues of arbitrariness and will.

My fascination with surprise—which is embedded in the history of philosophy and theology—led to the announcement of the inner antinomy of the church's feat and the indeterminacy of spiritual experience. Taking nothing for granted is the basis for reasoning, which is the criterion of both theory and practice. Anthropological experiences about sin as "repetition" and about originality as "uniqueness" have yielded several texts, in which I look back at the possible consequences of a too-easy confidence in the latest technological inventions.

In an essay dedicated to Dostoevsky, I ask the question about the need for this writer in the twenty-first century. This book comes to light at a moment when the greatest drama since the Second World War is taking place in the writer's wider homeland, sowing death, destruction, and misery. We are reminded again of the complexity of the "Russian soul" revealed in Dostoevsky's foolish heroes—those critics of absolutism, naked power, and the triumphalism of empire. In *The Russian Idea*, Berdyaev echoes this theme, asserting that when, for the Russians, a widely accepted idea cannot be realized, the outcome is a paradox, an antipodal result, or a tragic impasse.

Now, when all the signs confirm that something is ending on the international horizon and a new paradigm of life is emerging, we must not abandon the desire to illuminate the "meaning" of existence.

One of the essays is a review of an Athonite Elder's theology who, with an ease of expression and movement through ideas and topics, without a trace of deep breathing or insistence, presents before us a different theology from the ones we usually meet. It is theology as a surprise: a description of the personal experience of true Christians who dare to venture into the inner core of life (discourses, personalities, and problems) in order to both take that core out and preserve the intimacy of the gifted and seen.

I should like to express my warmest thanks to Teodora Gita Simić for translating the book from Serbian to English and to Basil (Sigurd) Lefsrud for his kindness and an invaluable assistance in reading and commenting on my manuscript.

By handing over these essays to readers, I express the hope that my humble thoughts will testify to both the original spirit of the Church and its realism.

Ostrog Monastery,
acrylic on canvas, 2021, Bishop Maxim

An eschatological rendering of the world. The Ostrog Monastery is situated against an almost vertical background, high up on the large rock of Ostroška Greda, in Montenegro.

DISCERNMENT INSPIRED BY THE FUTURE

"You must work spiritually not only until you see the fruit in your soul, but also until the very *end* (i.e., passing away). For even ripe fruit is often destroyed by hail," says the great Father Isaac the Syrian, bishop of Nineveh, who resigned from his position (as the Syrian historian Isho'dnah [9th century] recounts) "because of the envy of the inhabitants of the inland areas." Isaac's poetic sentence metaphorically stresses the need for vigilance and discernment as key requisites for achieving the goal of every effort. Premature rejoicing can be detrimental: we see it happen all the time in sports, political or church affairs, the economy, and other areas of life.

In our era of transhuman technology, characterized by a considerable lack of judgement, coupled with apparent inattentiveness, ascetical wisdom (e.g. the *Patericon*, the *Ladder of Divine Ascent*, etc.) is the best source of insightful advice for the modern man. Apart from being inattentive and unfocused (which is nothing to pride ourselves on), we humans are also disposed to often lose the horizon of expectation because our goals lack clarity. This in turn leads to spiritual, moral, social, cultural, and every other type of disorientation.

This topic becomes even more interesting considering that, as a rule, the Fathers of the Church lived in times of intense theological, philosophical and political debates, so the gift of discernment was crucial for determining spiritual direction and for clearly formulating the truths of the faith. For example, having lived in times of not only persistent dogmatic (Monophysitism, Monothelitism, etc.), but also political crises associated with the Muslim expansion into the Middle East, St. Maximus the Confessor (580-662), a peripatetic monk and prolific theologian, suffered accusations and slander throughout his life, for matters both of faith and practice. During a period of seven years he was tried twice in Constantinople (655 and 662), and tortured and forcibly exiled three times for resolute adherence to his teaching about the two wills and energies that are in Christ. Despite all of those adversities, however, Maximus resisted the temptation to reciprocate (i.e., to take revenge) on those who slandered him.

What was it that compelled the Church Fathers to refrain from passing judgment in those difficult times and to continue to fight? There are three common and interrelated terms that they used in relation to this topic: "crisis" (judgment, turning point), "diacrisis" (discernment, to sort) and "criterion" (measure, standard). In order to face and effectively overcome crisis through reasoning, it is necessary to have theological and spiritual *criteria* by which one can *discern* what constitutes a theologically legitimate viewpoint and what does not—that is, what *is* the very *esse* of the Church. In addition, in order to assess a critical situation, one must also have a vision of the future, i.e., what we know to be God's will for our future. It is manifest that this point—the relationship between the future and historical discernment—is central to the patristic teaching and practice of discernment.

How can I hate if love will last forever?

There are many aspects of patristic thought that show that only those things which are positive—such as love, the good, justice, etc.—have eschatological permanence, whereas those that are negative—such as division, hatred, malevolence, etc.—belong to the present age and will not survive in eternity. This simple truth helped Christians (lay people, monks, clergy) take a position that their behavior must reflect the life of the age to come and not contradict it. If there is no hate in eternity with Christ, then, they reasoned, we should do our best not to hate anyone. Similarly, the fact that there is no compromise between life and death led Christians to not fear death (the last enemy), for it was abolished. Sounds simple, does it not? Perhaps, but it does not end there. That is, until the anticipated End comes, we cannot be sure of anything. We still have serious labor and struggle ahead.

Crucial to our more robust understanding of discernment is the premise that all beings are endowed with "telos"—purpose or goal—and until the "telos" is realized we cannot speak about the "truth" of any being. Thus, it is reasoning about "the end." This raises questions of the will (freedom, self-determination) and drama (unavoidable in human history). In this respect, it should be emphasized that the Cross as both "judgment" and a test of commitment is the ultimate criterion for any assessment; the saints remained steadfast when confronted with the hardships of ascetic practice. Although a wide variety of terms can be used to describe the ascetic life, the Fathers use them from the eschatological perspective as well.

Maximus the Confessor, for instance, says that remembering only the bad things others do is a cruel form of discrimination which, in turn, prevents us from loving our brethren; whereas forgiveness leads to love even for our enemies, thus overcoming the "present age" in an "unnatural" way. With a personal example of forgiveness and discernment, this Confessor showed that he incorporated the future (love) into his life and way of reasoning. Love "entices the will to follow nature's ways and not swerve from the (eschatological) law of nature." Similar was the case of Symeon the New Theologian, who harbored no hatred or malice against the Metropolitan Stephen of Nicomedia. On the contrary, he said this to him: "I love you, Your Eminence, and I believe you love me too. You sent me to exile out of love ... and now I see the fruits of it, for I have anchored myself to the Rock (i.e.,

Christ), my feet are planted upon the Rock of Faith and will not falter! I thank you for this favor!"

This vision gives rise to the discernment that develops into "hermeneutics inspired by the future." That prudent *assessment* of present and past events in the light of the future is an important theological tool in the hands of the Church even today when faced with the current crisis of the meaning of life.

This sort of reasoning, thus, cannot ignore the vital needs of the modern man. Fr. Georges Florovsky formulated it with these sobering words: "The modern man can and should insist on the Tradition as well as on the Church of the Fathers as normative for the faith. But this does not exclude the right to *freedom* of opinion, nor does it mean we should disregard the needs and demands of the modern world." This perspective is far broader than a narrow shell of some *magisterium*, or a so-called *missio canonica* of the Church, which *missio*, after all, does not exist in Orthodox tradition. Florovsky did not hesitate to say that "servility (δουλικότητα) is alien both to the Bible and to the Fathers. They were themselves bold and courageous and adventurous seekers of the Divine truth." Resistance has always been the more preferable spiritual pathway than apathy.

"Christification" of everything

Theology could have arisen only out of that bold and limitless freedom in Christ—a theology that transforms peoples by baptizing them in the process. At the level of philosophy, important Aristotelian terms (such as τέλος, δύναμις, ἐνέργεια) have been adopted and have formed a distinct amalgam whereby the Hellenic (Aristotelian) metaphysics finds its natural place in biblical, eschatological theology. The Platonic notion of the soul, with due modifications and refinements, was adopted on the understanding that "neither soul nor body can exist in isolation, but are always the body and the soul not only of a given man, but of each and every man considered as a whole of which they remain parts," as formulated by the apologist Athenagoras. (In other words, neither soul nor body separately represents man.) Moreover, the belief in the natural immortality of the soul was considered heresy, more serious than the heresy of *thnetopsychism* (belief in the death of soul and body until resurrection). I would like to emphasize that it is precisely the method of discernment based on the future state ("I look for the resurrection of the dead"—only the whole man represents the truth about man) that has invalidated the claim that the Christian faith rests on the belief in the immortality of the soul.

In worship, however, many pagan customs have been adopted and Christianized (such as folk feasts, *slava*, and rituals). Something similar was done in the field of art where the great artistic achievements of antiquity were embraced and incorporated into the Christian artistic heritage, which is reflected in the richness and diversity of forms, techniques and expressions. In some cases, this symbiosis created some "tension" (like the status of philosophical concepts in theology), but it originated from the intention of both preserving valuable elements (like Aristotelian teleology and metaphysics) and fusing them with the Judeo-Christian *eschatology of the resurrection*. This process did not lead to the "Hellenization of Christianity" but to the "Christianization of Hellenism."

All of this together represents today the *Tradition* that generations of Christians weaved into the fabric of the church. One contemporary father of the Church intimates what *Tradition is* when he notes that the Virgin "treasured all Christ's sayings in her heart" (cf. Luke 2:19; 2:51). In this way, entirely new artistic and intellectual works have been created throughout history, not dictated by nature but by *freedom*. In Florovsky's terms, freedom can overcome necessity and even reverse the laws of nature in the light of the coming Kingdom—as the martyrs and ascetics of the Church witness. In this sense, Christians did not base their understanding of the future on the belief in the immortality of the soul (which was a ready-made, platonic solution of that time) but on their faith in the "community of the saints," which is the Church as the Body of Christ, experienced in the Eucharist. Thus, the Christology of the resurrection solves the conundrum of life. This, however, is neither obvious nor predictable, but comes as a surprise from the future, as a *revelation* or a gift. There can be no discernment without revelation—or it is nothing but pure human inventiveness. Therefore, in the words of Climacus, "a discerning man finds health and destroys sickness."

Ignorance (ἀμάθεια) and *passion* (ἐμπάθεια) are the two main characteristics of today's world. When we combine our metaphysical illiteracy with a passionate desire to eliminate those who do not think like us, we only create confusion and discontent around us. This is because (we think to ourselves) only *our* myopic perspective is correct, and it should therefore dominate all other perspectives. We advance a single perspective that does not allow for alternatives. One then forgets that there is no justifiable *necessity* for the "dichotomy" between Jerusalem (the simple, gospel faith) and Athens (the Hellenic philosophical synthesis), between the West (a culture based on the ancient Greek and Judeo-Christian culture) and the East (on whose soil the Orthodox live and act), between theology (the word of God) and science (the study of the laws of nature). On the contrary, one realizes that only creative encounter and interaction will enrich the world in which we live together. Prayer for the peaceful coexistence of God's nations, tribes, languages and cultures never ceases in the Church. Nor does prayer for our reconciliation in the One Body of the Church throughout the world.

By His incarnation, the Lord was enthroned and "robed in *beauty*" of the human person and cosmic creation (which was contaminated with sin, corruption, suffering and mortality). By professing this truth, we believe that 21st century theology will not fall into the same trap as the Inquisition, provided that theologians—following the advice of Abba Isaac—practice their faith and live a life of self-surrender and self-sacrifice.

***Christos Yannaras*,**
acrylic on canvas, 2021, Bishop Maxim

"Yannaras has radically renewed the cultural perception of religious discourse by the force and novelty of his thinking and by the style of his linguistic expression. He has an imposing presence on the Greek cultural scene. It is no exaggeration to say that one can easily distinguish between pre-Yannaras and post-Yannaras theology in Greece, between theology as an academic discipline and theology as a passion for the fullness of life, for victory over death."

(Basilio Petra)

THE FLAME IN OUR LADY'S HAIR

Paris is not merely a place, it is also a "way of life," said the Athenian theologian and philosopher Christos Yannaras. And a way of life is always the result of *how* (the manner in which) things exist. At the onset of this millennium, Catherine Dolez, a professor at the Alliance Française, persistently argued that the term *laïcité* has became a necessary complement to a tripartite motto *liberté, égalité, fraternité.* I endeavored to make her also consider *koinos logos* (Heraclitus' "general, common cause") as fundamental to the essential identity of the *polis.* How can a city be called a city unless it has a constant point of reference that brings all to the same place? In response, she wrote an entire essay claiming that the identity of Paris is based precisely on the absence of an underlying *logos.* On April 15, 2019, however, events revealed that this city nevertheless does have a fundamental point of reference that makes it coherent: a deep attachment to Notre Dame de Paris. It was expressed *unexpectedly,* for a moment only, but strongly enough to point to that forgotten *way, un véritable mode d'existence.* The French watched in horror as their magnificent and emblematic cathedral of Our Lady of Paris burned before their eyes. They were scared of losing their own selves, their identity. The fire caught the Virgin's hair, but, fortunately, it did not consume it. *That* fire, though, came at just the right time.

The value and importance that Notre Dame holds over every French person (and beyond) is unfathomable. President Macron stated something that needed no explanation: "We have lost part of our lives, of our destiny." Victor Hugo considered Notre Dame an asylum and wanted to preserve it as such, *inviolable*. The church of the Mother of God in this metropolis is a symbol of past epochs preserved by Hugo as we follow the unfortunate fates of Quasimodo, the "hunchback of Notre Dame," Esmeralda, the corrupt archdeacon Claude Frollo and other characters. (To this generation that reads fewer and fewer books I recommend the 1996 Walt Disney animated film based on Hugo's novel).

In a way, Paris *is* the city of Our Lady, just as Los Angeles was at one time (*Nuestra Señora Reina de los Ángeles*, founded in early 1784), Prizren with its Church of the Holy Mother of Eleusa (*Bogorodica Ljeviška*, Our Lady of Tenderness) and Constantinople on the Bosphorus. Notre Dame is breathtaking. Dating from the 12th century, it is a masterpiece with its flying buttresses, stunning stained-glass windows, carved gargoyles and fantastical creatures. Inside its walls are priceless relics, paintings, statues and other precious artifacts. The exterior of the church has been the subject of countless paintings and drawings as well as literary works.

Stone-carved images to the glory to God

In his column in the Sunday issue (July 27, 2020) of the newspaper *Kathimerini* on Notre Dame, Christos Yannaras effectively demonstrated that the fire on the roof of the cathedral started an inexplicable surge of admiration for its architectural wonders even in those who knew very little about them. We know that France is a society that once (under known circumstances) chose to define itself as "atheistic" (e.g. professor Dolez clearly stated that *laïcité* meant "without religion"). How is it possible that Notre Dame—the second principal church of Western Christianity, formidably imposing on that little island in the Seine—is part of the very "being" of the French whereas at the same time they claim that their mode of being is "atheistic"? Yannaras wondered whether instead of Macron saying that Notre Dame was their history, their literature, their imagination, it would have been more appropriate and consistent to admit that Notre Dame was in fact the spiritual womb that *gave birth* to them, which they later *jettisoned*. And then he continued, and I paraphrase, "because we, French, created a different culture, a different way of life, we wore glasses that did not allow us to recognize why we are so profoundly touched by this cathedral of Notre Dame." The leading Christian philosopher of Europe (as Rowan Williams calls Yannaras) added insightfully: "We look superficially at things, and where stone-masons carved images to the glory to God, we admire the aesthetics and monumentality, discounting the fervent love that gave birth to that beauty."

In another of his works, writing about Byzantine and Gothic architecture, Yannaras pointed out that both built temples with *faith*. "The same people who built Gothic cathedrals also produced theological *Summae*," said Marie-Dominique Chenu. According to Yannaras, "undoubtedly, the appearance of magnificent Gothic-style cathedrals was the first technological application of scholastic thought, indicative of a technological relationship to the natural building materials and a stunning artistic expression of the autarchic and sentimental imposition of ecclesiastical power and magnificence." Indeed, the history of architecture is the history of writing. Before the printing press, mankind communicated through architecture. From Stonehenge to the Parthenon, alphabets were inscribed in "books of stone." Rows of stones were sentences, Hugo insists, while Greek columns were "hieroglyphs" pregnant with meaning. The stone-masons of old kissed every stone before laying them in the wall.

The French Senate has voted to ensure that Notre-Dame de Paris be rebuilt to look just as it did before the fire. Yannaras notices the paradox that flows from the determination to rebuild Notre Dame "using a technology that allows for remarkable imitations, as our culture today is based on impressions, not on a realism of relations." The reason it will be rebuilt is because this "monument" continues to impress 13 million visitors every year. "We do not have master builders, that very soul of the Art, but we have money and machines that are only able to produce, untiringly, ... imitations!"

Why does our Athenian lover of wisdom lament over the hypocrisy of our time? Because in so many places in the world only a faint glow can be seen where once shone a brilliant light of the *polis* of ancient democracy and the Christian *ecclesia*. "People uneducated in the essentials of culture have never wondered which metaphysics gave birth to the Parthenon, tragedy, democracy, Hagia Sophia, eucharistic dramaturgy, *demos* as a self-governing community free from external pressures." Those who still today do not ask themselves about the *cause* and *purpose* of existence cannot recognize Art as the fruit of faith and inventiveness. "Today, art has been reduced to a commodity (commercial gratification) or has degenerated into sheer utilitarianism," says Yannaras.

Metaphysical illiteracy

We may lament with Yannaras that this saddening "metaphysical illiteracy" is also a feature of America's overall social decadence, individualism, amorality, and non-communication (i.e., willingness to readily exclude and excommunicate others) that so blatantly dominates virtually every segment of our own fractured *ethos*. Even church events, even parishes and dioceses—once likened to an ecclesiastical hive of bees—have ceased to concern themselves with the realities of today's world and have become, as a rule, overly preoccupied with petty formalities (e.g. how one speaks, walks, stands, or gestures, what one looks at, etc.). Our everyday social life is marked by absolute declarations and banal statements, by moralizing and preaching. Is an ecclesiastical event in today's Orthodox Church true eucharistic communion in the fullest sense, as the body of the faithful gathered together in a relationship of mutual love, which the Apostle Paul so poignantly speaks about? Or has it also turned into a formality, into ideological statements, and into an invitation to pragmatic orthopraxy? The way of approaching truth has become either overly rational or sentimental (that is, individualistic), and "salvation" has turned into dry legalism and petty egocentrism.

Our Lady that "burns yet is untouched by the flames" invites us all to come out of the seductive self-sufficiency of authority and self-proclaimed power elite that expects gifts and approval, applause and flattering. From beneath the ashes and rubble of ideological ruins shines forth the Paschal proclamation that *death was trampled down by death.* The decoding of the gospel narratives should not employ the method of reasoning common to today's sermons and statements. With an inaudible voice, the gospel has already shattered the night as the dawn of the mysterious Day draws near. Nothing can defeat that gospel. Hemingway put these words in the Old Man's mouth as a lesson to one boy: "You see, they can beat you, but they cannot defeat you." The same Hemingway also wrote: "If you are lucky enough to have lived in Paris as a young man, then wherever you go for the rest of your life, it stays with you, for Paris is a moveable feast." And what about Notre Dame? Its feast day of the Mother of God is the vigil kept ceaselessly in the Church, a moveable feast as a life-long ascent (or descent) until the dawning of the day of Pascha itself. For "in time she ineffably conceived and gave birth to the Timeless God," as we chant in the Church's liturgy.

My Foundations are in the Mountains (***Elder Vasileios of Iveron** in Sedona, Arizona, 2012*), acrylic on canvas, 2022, Bishop Maxim

Through a well-designed environment, the absolute value of the image is projected—the face. It seems to have come out of the hands of the illustrator very easily and simply, although it transparently expresses deep existential concerns. The skin of the face, despite some wrinkles, is calm and smooth, expressing the kindness of Fr. Vasileios. His two eyes express a sacred adolescence, an endless in-depth exploration of the meaning of the infinite beauty of the landscape for the meaning of the world, for the future of the world. It is as if he is telling us: "Give me all the worlds, bring me all the graces of nature, my soul thirsts for the One! The Divine Love of Christ!" It is indeed a portrait of a real monk, who is chosen by nature but longs for the Kingdom of heaven.

AN ATHONITE ELDER'S THEOLOGY OF SURPRISE

For in the realm of truth, repetition is surprise.
Elder Vasileios of Iveron

Anyone who has read *Selected Writings* of Archimandrite Vasileios[1] can understand the author's desire for all of us who live and struggle in this wounded world to became aware of and uphold the spiritual nobility and dignity of human beings—which implies that to be human is to be a child of God, a free person and a priest of creation. We are therefore called (by name) to transition from non-being to all-being, since "this calling by name is a mystical lightning flash that illuminates hitherto unknown dimensions of human existence." Let us listen to this gentle Elder. Let us who are chasing health and fitness in gyms and on treadmills (where one keeps running but gets nowhere), at any cost and in step with the beat of the modern world, see in this a metaphor for life without aim. He speaks to us the saving words that our successes do not belong to a domain that is subject to decay (stained with the cold sweat of fear and disillusionment) but in the abolition of death, which, in turn, tells us that "physical health cannot save us, nor can a disease kill us."

[1] Elder Vasileios, *Selected Writings* (Alexander Press: Montréal, QC & Sebastian Press: Alhambra, 2022).

To all of us who have degenerated the deafening, yet silent word of the Gospel to the insipid rhetoric, lifeless epistemology and (all too often) pseudo-problematics—so that we no longer have the joy of life needed to "sing a new song," nor are we receptive to the rhythms and frequencies of the Resurrection earthquake—his writing comes as a breath of fresh air, refreshing as the dews of Hermon. This dew can bring us a little joy that laughs at death, it can remove the world's soot that has built up all around, it can remove the coverings (manners and routines) that suffocate us and it can disperse the mist of ignorance. The Elder's writing style is different, representing an antidote to the anemic piety of our days and bearing witness to the transcendent. Having passed through dark places and tasted the Passover of the future, his writing exudes the scent of sanctity and teaches the logic of the Age to come. Such a person (not being a moralist) is not troubled by the actions of the weak, since he recognizes the stifled pain of the delicate soul of a fallen man that cries for help.

Yes, this is about Vasileios Gondikakis, the pro-Hegumen (and for many years Abbot) of Iveron Monastery on the Holy Mountain. His *Selected Writings* are wonderfully unusual books, difficult to describe. We can nevertheless recognize in them the distinct characteristics of the natural and earnest tone he uses when he speaks about God and man.

The code that reconciles the opposites

The essence of the theological synthesis of Vasileios of Iveron can be found in three areas. Firstly, in his systematic review of human achievements in history that includes the greatest thinkers from ancient Hellenic philosophers to modern Western writers. Next, he supports the hermeneutics of the Resurrection, although in a way that is, admittedly, overburdened with idiosyncratic language and semantics. And finally, in his "theology of surprise." All three draw from Church tradition and are deeply ecclesiastical in nature.

As for the first area, Vasileios is known for combining seemingly opposing elements ("pure" logicians can be deterred by this). He is a writer who expresses his views on the subject of human life freely, using quotes from works written by writers from the East and the West as he deems appropriate, as if they were not separated by different cultures and traditions: Heraclitus, Abba Isaac, Albert Camus, Apostle Paul, Fyodor Dostoevsky, Stefan Zweig, Porphyrios the Kapsokalyvite, et al. Having discovered the "code" that unites them, he moves with ease in the company of those luminaries who pushed creativity to new heights (though only after having previously delved into the depths of our common nature). He says that the latter, Porphyrios, "refreshed and cheered the heart of the twentieth century with his divine smile." At the same time, he understands that the salvation of men and the world are not two separate realities. The salvation of the cosmos and the calling of man "by name," go hand in hand towards the adoption of man by God and the redemption of creation. Salvation, moreover, has the dimension of a *loss*—the grain that *dies* brings fort much fruit, and the most beautiful of those fruits is love for all creatures. He tells us that no one but a saint can "receive more cordially and embrace more willingly all the mischievous children of history" (like Isaac the Syrian with whom he frequently keeps company). He knows that while Heraclitus condemned the idols of wisdom and poetry, orgies, blood sacrifices, and deemed it nonsensical to pray to statues, the Elder Porphyrios condemned pretended holiness, sycophantic obedience and feigned humility as demonic illusions.

The defining narratives of his books are obscured by a multitude of compelling details but, overall, they are genuinely honest, although occasionally somewhat confusing. His theological *word* (logos) is suggestive, honest and responsible, and he is open to all topics "since the last word of the God-Logos has not yet been uttered." Thus, he sharpens our senses so that we can be prepared for all has not yet been revealed, for in the universe of the Church's theology there are bright stars of truth whose light has not yet reached us. It is no wonder that the Elder, in order to convey the unspeakable, inevitably expresses himself both *cataphatically* and *apophatically* (i.e., he speaks in positives and negatives, since he is familiar with both) and sometimes even *clairvoyantly* (and it seems that this is a conscious choice). For example, he uses and re-uses fragments of expressions, concepts and images in new and unanticipated combinations. What is apparent is his effortless command of language which, while not lacking in accuracy of description or variety of rhythms, is expressive and melodious. In his philosophy we see *an ultimate existentialism* (i.e., a concern with the ultimate, eschatological) as his interests are geared toward the immense problems of life. We also see that his key to the door of truth is in the Resurrection. Thus, a torrent of inspiration springs forth effortlessly from his genius.

A welcome encouragement

The *language* of the Iveronian Elder is unusual, even "oxymoronic," because, in the manner of psalms, he is at once the sender and the receiver of the message of an extraordinary "supra-contextual" life. It is therefore possible for him to speak about the same topic over and again without repeating himself, and without falling into the trap of stereotypes or clichés. For, to use his own words, "in the realm of truth, each repetition is a surprise." His elliptical sentences do not aspire to a poetic eloquence that would tickle one's ears, but they do help to avoid a one-sided positivism. He expresses poetically and laconically the theme of "sober intoxication," and wisely, because (being a shrewd observer) he perceives an abyss as a bridge and an insurmountable mountain as a gentle plain, and can therefore move forth without obstacles. Sometimes he may appear to be too harsh on those who play the game of being "objective," never exposing themselves to uncomfortable situations, let alone sacrifice and suffering. That is why they are advised that they must become intoxicated by the madness of love, their mind transformed in a wholesome way, if they want to gain the true meaning of life and wisdom. He tells us that we can think of theology as a two-lane road, one *ascending* and the other *descending*. On this point we should heed his advice. After the Transfiguration, the teaching of the Lord continues no longer by ascending "to the high mountain" in order to look at His divine glory, but by descending to suffering humanity. The perfect image of this is the Holy Liturgy in which we experience both comings of Christ. "The Future Age (τὰ ἔσχατα) should not be construed in narrow temporal terms, which is future, for even today it illuminates history and creation through liturgy."

To those in *power* (secular or religious), the following message is especially important: It is not by negating the other that we become free of him. If we relinquish the other person, one cannot forget that the other still possesses the "power" and ability to move forward freely, "through closed doors," and may visit us, causing a feeling of uneasiness. This feeling will last until we realize that salvation and resurrection of the other take place in our heart and in our life—and that their life is also streaming through our being. Flowers do not open into full bloom in ice-cold winter time, but in the warmth of spring; likewise, one cannot open one's heart when facing threats, but only in a climate of love, when an atmosphere of trust prevails. For love is not sentimentality, but sacrifice.

The astonishing density of thought of this wise man and his power of suggestion can be compared to advice given by experienced physicians. "You have chosen a sacred and priestly profession, which puts you in a tragically privileged position. You get to see people at the most challenging and sacred moments of their lives. May God help you prove yourself worthy of your mission." The recommendation to always give a divinely inspired diagnosis is even more applicable to spiritual fathers. He gives *bishops* encouraging advice to beware of yielding to that seductive self-sufficiency of authority and autarchic power which expects to be showered with gifts, praise, and adulation. For those, the full meaning of the Elder's words can be found in this sentence: "Listen to that voice of the Shepherd that echoes in your ears, sweetens your heart, and permeates your soul like the rain poured on the thirsty land." It is as if he is saying: Dear Bishop, you must provide the field of your diocese with the care of the Shepherd "who seeks the lost," and with the mercy of a Samaritan who "pours wine and oil on the injured men." Then you will gain new strength and in the advanced years of episcopal service your youth will be renewed like the eagle's, precisely because everything is overflowing with love for God's creation. Then you will draw everyone to Christ and the Church, not to *your* authority and virtue. He advises you, my brother Bishop, not to swirl into the fervor of a passionate dispute: "Rebuke those who contradict you by the power of your virtues, not by your words." As to the *monks*, he gives them discerning and laconic advice (together with Isaac the Syrian): "Get to know the intricacies of your mind by the kind of temptations you experience."

And to the *youth*, he says that since we all need to achieve what is unattainable, we all need the *courage of faith*, which is an integral part of the human being. "Just as we need oxygen to live in this life, so do we need the power of faith to live eternal life." And he gives us practical advice for our *digital* age: "With the development of science, technology and especially electronics, many dangerous and uncontrollable possibilities have been given to man, which exceed his spiritual maturity level and awareness." Vasileios reminds us of the time when the sacred texts were created: "They were written in another time, in another space: in a deeply human and desirable space, from which, however, we have willfully or inadvertently distanced away, and threw ourselves into that foreign land of machinery and industry, where when something humbles itself, it ceases to exist."

Nostalgia for a new language

It is consoling that this Athonite monk speaks to us in a language that reveals but does not revile or belittle.

"Those who want to keep their power position will suffer. They will not be able to hide a disease that eats from the inside. When praised by others, such persons will start to flatter themselves to the point of delusion, and become saddened to the point of despair when their self-image is threatened or disturbed." And then he confides in us that the burning of a saintly heart "melts the entire creation," creating conditions for "the dough of your life and creativity to rise when leavened with the yeast of the Kingdom which is to come."

Why is this approach important and where does it lead? It is important because, on the one hand, it satisfies our nostalgia for authentic theology, and, on the other hand, it points to the problem related to the way we talk about God, man and the world. With the help of a "hermeneutics of the Resurrection," Vasileios of Iveron helps decipher the problems of the biblical and patristic tradition. The truth cannot only destroy death and make present the glory of the Eighth Day, but it can also liberate us from the spell of falsehood and illusion (hence the prophetic mission and responsibility of Christians). God does not act in obvious ways ("His own brothers did not believe in Him"), but God's acts throughout history have had a constant *factor of surprise,* in the sense that the Lord's presence is like the sudden flash of lightning that illuminates everything under heaven. For those who are touched by the Truth, "his being, like a magnetized needle, is unwaveringly drawn to the Northern Star that many do not know much about." And then, like Columbus, "you set sail into the endless ocean in search of a new world that your soul longs for." Remember, though, that to live by the logic of the Resurrection means to live within the *icon* of the Resurrection, in Hades where Christ has descended. "That icon is representative of your life. Christ will keep pulling you out with His hand, taking you to the light, to freedom, to an endless journey, which is He Himself." And then, perhaps, while you are being pulled out to the light, you will grab someone else's hand...

You will notice, dear reader, how Vasileios interweaves poetry and logic, canonical instructions and anecdotes, aesthetics and ecology, metaphysics and biblical exegesis. Behind the charm and intricacy of this panoptic approach, however, a potential vulnerability is hidden. It is one thing to quote a beautiful passage from the *Patericon* or to invoke an inspired saying of an ancient Syrian writer, but it is another (and more demanding) thing to *show* that such texts are relevant to us—that we can deduce from them what kinds of decisions we should make in our time and society, and what kind of lives we should lead. The composition of his essays, at the same time episodic but solid in texture, is reminiscent of Heraclitus' writing style. With such an approach, *faith* and *knowledge* are one and the same thing. As such, it becomes clear that the leitmotif of his whole oeuvre is that ascetics "undergo things divine rather than thinking about them." For he who lives in Christ, for whom the end of the ages has already arrived, sees everything as pure and serene, because "to the pure all things are pure."

By what measure can one evaluate his theology in academic terms? The suggestive power and high degree of descriptive refinement of Gondikakis' theological idiosyncrasy is beyond doubt. What is unclear at first glance is its status in terms of credibility. One could say that much of his theology is not based on a scientifically demonstrable corpus of facts but on the imagination of an individual genius and on the circumstances of its formation (the unique atmosphere of Mount Athos). In response to this objection, I would say that an important consequence of such an endeavor is the unpredictability of statements that stems from the unpredictability of a spiritual experience that is far from static. In other words, it was this experience that produced a *theology of surprise*. What are the characteristics of this theology? First, its epistemology does not narrow the horizon of research, but rather opens it, as it feeds on surprise and anticipation. This is not an idiom of pseudoscience without a shred of substance in its claims and evidence. Further, recognizing these *ultimate human existential concerns* is not as simple as it might seem at first glance. (For example, someone could say, if you look thorough blue lenses, everything will appear blue.) Also, it does not limit our options, because "what is true is also truly polysemous with innumerable applications and surprising connections."

It can be said that precisely because of the "epistemology of the resurrection," some of the little things in life (gestures, voices, sounds, analogies) that previously did not mean a lot—because we were probably affected by an illusion of self-sufficiency, accompanied by indifference and insensitivity—begin to speak volumes. In the field of human relations, our eyes are opened in a Christ-like way: "If you do not see Christ in the face of the stranger, the sick, the oppressed, the outcast, then you do not know Him at all." After all, those who faithfully adopt this hermeneutic will not only "speak in new tongues" but "will lay hands on the sick and they shall recover." And they will be surprised at that gift, the same way they were surprised to see that the repentant thief became the first inhabitant of Paradise. Therefore, to live by the logic of the Resurrection does not mean to remove all doubts and never feel pain. To the contrary, within this logic everything becomes precious, and the whole can be seen in the smallest of details. But "a person with such a sensibility always has Someone who keeps him company, and He Himself, with His entire being, is friends with everyone." And so the companionship continues. "He is with you wherever you are. You recognize Him and love Him as the great, most holy, and eternal Passover." In this new context of life, "there is nothing that can become habitual. Everything is a refreshingly peaceful surprise, the birth of light that is life and salvation of the world. Everything is nourished by only one source of consolation that, one can sense it inside, unites everything." What is required in patristic study, in order to remain faithful to the Fathers' spirit of freedom and worthy of their spiritual nobility and freshness, is to approach their holy texts with the awe in which we approach and venerate the holy relics and icons.

This Hagiorite reminds us that Christians whose hope is in Christ "long for what we already have and remember what we expect." He speaks about Him as someone "madly in love." Anyone who looks at a photograph of young Vasileios from Crete (mid-last century) will see the same joy of life and angelic countenance of a child ... who, even in his earliest years, displayed diverse and broad interests in Saint Sophia, Europe and Orthodoxy, medicine, physics, Olympic games, icons of Theophanes the Cretan, the Athonite concept of space and time, Hollywood film.

The works of the Elder are replete with oxymorons, but they are not absurd statements and artificial metaphorical constructs, rather (as I see them) biblical, characteristic expressions of the Areopagitic linguistic paradoxes of the Truth that likes to hide. For example, by His Ascension into heaven, Christ becomes "invisible" precisely so that His disciples would not lose sight of Him. When the hour came for Him to appear among his fellow travelers to Emmaus, (after they had suffered great effort and pain of body and mind), and as they finally recognized who He was, He became invisible again. Why? Because "by becoming invisible to the sensual, He is revealed to the spiritual eye ... He continues to live in them inseparably forever."

At the remote skete of Iveron at the foot of Mt. Athos, in the great silence of the Holy Mountain, pervaded with the scent of conifers and wild meadow flowers and refreshed by the sea breeze that brings the "ozone" of health, the Elder Vasileios lives and works. Unpretentiously and authentically, he seeks to bring back to life what must have once been the deepest transformative change in the process of knowledge acquisition, brought about by scriptural and patristic epistemology. This brings us divine comfort, "serenity without serenity." And it puts within each one of us the spark of eternal life so that in the confusion of modern urban life we can recognize the elements of peace and security. Vasileios encourages us, while at the same time letting us be free, "to see the wonderful in the smallest of things, in the momentarily eternal now, and feed our souls on the warmth of eternal love that immortalizes that which is transient." In the final analysis, it is within the heart that a Christian believes and "glorifies the two comings of the Lord that have come together in one place."

I can already hear the theologians of the future speaking in a *new tongue* that reflects the immediacy of real-life experience. I hope that they will be able to provide godly guidance in their communities and that their service will give comfort and encouragement to those on the narrow path that leads to the Door of Life.

***Fr. Alexander Schmemann**: Paschal Eucharist*,
acrylic on canvas, 2022, Bishop Maxim

At Pascha, during the service before the closed doors of the chapel, many would notice how his face would entirely transfigure and be full of light. Alexander Dmitrievich Schmemann (1921-1983) was an influential Orthodox priest, theologian, and author who spent most of his career in the United States. Born in Estonia to émigrés from the Russian Revolution, he grew up primarily in France, where there was a large émigré community in Paris.

St. Justin of Chelie, acrylic on canvas, Paris, 2004,
Stamatis Skliris and Bishop Maxim

St. Justin created a new theological and philosophical language powerfully reaching the heart of the contemporary human being. His writings and teachings reflect a genuine and total commitment to Christ. He was "living dogma" and a "flute of the Spirit" reflecting the divine love of God the Holy Trinity. Theology was life to St. Justin.

REPETITION OF SIN AND INNOVATION OF THE SPIRIT

When the Apostle Paul reminded the Christians in Galatia that they became children of God through Christ, he also rebuked them for certain faults and vices: "How is it you are *turning again* to the weak and impoverished *elementals* (τά ἀσθενῆ καί πτωχά στοιχεῖα), for which you wish anew to *slave again*?" (Gal. 4:9). There is something profound and heart-rending about our fallen state: sin, like addiction, is a *repetition* of a certain experience. *Pathos* as an attachment to pleasure leads into a vicious cycle of repetition (of a single act) according to an established pattern. Addiction, psychologists say, is propelled by this desire to repeat a pleasure. The mechanism of sin has long been described in the context of a fallen (natural) state structured into three parts: pleasure-pain-punishment. (This is why the canons of the Church Fathers recommend the *epitimion*, some form of therapeutic penance, even if one accepts one's guilt: nature itself dictates a period of recovery through atonement). Because of the distinctive pattern, the ascetic fathers described the *genealogy* of passion and sin as an act of *repetition*, and almost "decoded" it to a degree that modern psychology can only envy. In contrast, no one has "deciphered" the state of grace and holiness, since there is no established order, pattern or stereotype of divine action (it is sufficient for grace to allow one to manifest love and freedom by faith and *repentance*). "The Spirit respires *where it will,* and you hear its sound, but you do not know *where it comes from* or *where it goes*: such is everyone born of the Spirit" (John 3:8). In interpreting this passage, Abba Justin of Ćelije notes succinctly: "It is *impossible* to measure or *categorize* the Spirit." Each blessing is unique, open to the future, whereas sin is *stereotypical* in nature and there is nothing unpredictable about it.

I often wonder if a "blind repetition" of the same procedure is some kind of *addictive* behavior? Repetition is not necessarily a bad thing, but sin, as a rule, is repetitive. For example, in the case of Don Juan, sin is repulsively *repetitive.* The subject is so challenging that Kierkegaard, in his philosophical novella under the distinctive name "Repetition" (1843), expanded the word into a philosophical concept. Religions are said to be *cultures of repetition.* In them, originality (or *novelty*) is *non grata.* This is evidenced by the fact that Loyola, Muhammad, Luther and others were overwhelmed by the *rules.* Innovation, on the other hand, is connected with the idea of freedom: The Christian God creates absolutely *new* things because he is free from concepts and models. Christ makes all things *new* (Rev. 21:5). *Mutatis mutandis,* a Christian introduces a novelty only when he is free. *Schematism* leads to *schism,* so Abba Justin warned in his personal notes:

"Every attempt to schematize life implies a schism (= schematism) of some kind, fracture, faction; chunks, fragments..."

There certainly is something guileless about slavish imitation of, for example, the style of icon painting, or chanting church music while following or adhering to a certain "canon." The freedom to not improvise can also be a virtue, while the desire to be original *at any cost* is characteristic of immature souls. On the other hand, the icons that we revere most—such as Our Lady of Vladimir, or Our Lady of Hilandar—are completely *different* from each other. Does that not suggest that something unusual is at play here? The archetype in itself is an unrepeatable original. And the person who copies the original work should know that they can never create an exact copy of what is in front of them, no matter how hard they try to faithfully reproduce every detail.

Poor copies of the fake originals

The phenomenon of *copying* and/or *originality* raises nothing less than the question of the fundamental right to imagination and creativity. From copyists in popular culture, to imitators in ecclesiastical culture, the same process is repeated: a slavish imitation that oftentimes leads to caricature. Having become a new "religion," Hollywood has taken from it a culture of repetition: countless fans strive to resemble the "stars," but they are nothing but poor copies of the fake originals. Cosmetics and technology allow for almost limitless replication, even in the field of genetics. Note that the *imitatio Christi* psychological model has never been developed in the East. (For the Apostle Paul, the imitation of Christ implies a willingness to *incline the mind* to the things of the Spirit—Rom. 8:4 and 8:8—or self-giving in the service to others in *love*—1 Cor. 13, Gal. 5:13 and Eph. 5:1).

If there were no past, of course, there would be no tradition which makes the ancient as alive in the Church as the present. When authentic, tradition is *avant-garde*, a precursor to future events. In such successful cases, one has difficulty discerning whether the new is more "classic" than the old. To rely *solely* on the past not only gives rise to painful romanticism but also leads to the drying up of creative impulses. Conversely, in describing authentic tradition Abba Justin of the Ćelije Monastery boldly used words like "immeasurable, above reason, above knowledge, unfathomable, undefinable, clairvoyant" for "such is everyone born of the Spirit." Indeed, "wherever the Spirit is there is freedom" (2 Cor. 3:17).

Is it still possible today—in our digital age where originals can be *multiplied* indefinitely—to be original? It seems that personal charisma no longer has a future precisely because there is no place in the polycentric world for real *dialogue*. If something does not change, we can forget about seeing among us new individual geniuses (like Plato, Shakespeare, Hegel, Einstein, Tesla...)! In their place, the latest fad gives us a so-called *collective brain*: everyone contributes to the general knowledge base, but personal originality is lost in the collective. Why is this so? Due to lack of time, perhaps? Today's super-fast flow of information does not leave us enough time to contemplate and evaluate ideas (let alone time to pray). Ideas require time, and we do not have the *time*. Thus, individuals gathered around virtual forums function as a *collective brain*, selectively conveying and absorbing information, usually detached from their own awareness. At one time, readers eagerly waited for a sequel to Dostoevsky's novel to come out, or for a new book by Jean Daniélou to appear, speculating about its content. The anticipation was palpable. Few people expect such things today: one hears about something, but it gets forgotten by the next day because one hears about something else new. All this causes that which is *unique* to be pushed to the background. If the Messiah appeared in history *today*, who would accept Him and for how long? How would the Sermon on the Mount be received? In what way would the Holy Spirit prepare the heart and mind of man to hear and *receive* the Gospel?

Wisdom lost in knowledge and information

The Internet seems to have become perhaps the last (?) expression of the collective nature of human intelligence. At the same time, the insatiable satiety of information suppresses both knowledge and wisdom, as the poet Thomas Eliot prophetically predicted. Today, language software can produce better work than students with high honors. One AI (Artificial Intelligence) research company has created a language model which generates meaningful paragraphs of text and achieves state-of-the-art performance on many language modeling benchmarks—offering rudimentary reading comprehension, machine translation, question answering and summarization—all without task-specific training. According to the British *Guardian*, the creators of this revolutionary AI system, which is allegedly capable of generating new stories and novels, have taken the unusual step of not making their research public, motivated by concern of possible misuse. *OpenAI*, the corporation governed by Elon Musk, Sam Altman, Reid Hoffman and others, claims that the new AI model, called GPT-2, is so good that the risk of abuse is very real, and therefore they are withholding its release in order to have more time to discuss the future of this latest technological breakthrough.

The vital question, however, is how will *OpenAI* provide a *new* angle of reflection? How will it take us where we have not been and say to us, "Here, look from this angle!" and genuinely surprise us!

The connection between "temporality" and "unexpected events" is exciting. The writer of the Areopagite texts[1] addresses the concept of "sudden" by ex-

[1] Dionysius the Areopagite (or Dionysius the Pseudo-Areopagite) was a Christian theologian and Neoplatonic philosopher of the late

plaining exactly what the biblical term ἐξαίφνης means. "*Sudden* is that which, contrary to expectation, and out of the, as yet, unmanifest, is brought into the manifest." Of course, he is referring to Christ as the God-man who, even after his incarnation, even after revealing himself, remains not fully revealed ("that hidden mystery of Jesus is in itself ineffable by word and unintelligible by reason").

In order to be able to recognize the original, it is necessary to step away from the familiar and known. In the moment of the "sudden" leap (*exaiphnes*), "the things that surround me must retreat and indeed 'disappear' in order to allow that which-is-not-manifest to show itself," writes Fr. John Manoussakis. Thus, "sudden" surprise will come to those who are not attached to "things," to those who patiently endure the cross of trials and afflictions of history, who see troubles as blessings and condemn no one: they are long-suffering, they do not envy, they are not proud, they do not do what is wrong, they do not seek their own, they are not irritated, they do not rejoice in injustice, and they rejoice with the truth, they tolerate everything, they have faith in all things, they hope in all things (1 Cor. 13: 5-7). Then, *unexpectedly* and without any *external* cause, as Abba Isaac says, the grace of God comes. What is faith if not an openness to the extraordinary? However, what if *transhumanism* oblit-

5th to early 6th century, who wrote a set of works known as the *Corpus Areopagiticum* or *Corpus Dionysiacum*.

erates this "openness of being," and even more than that, the ek-stasis of being?

The central objective of transhumanism[2] is to accelerate the evolution of humanity so radically that at the end of the process, humanity as such would disappear. The sovereign self here craves omniscience and omnipotence. The unconscious temptation underlying this desire is "why am I not a god?"

Since machines hold for the psyche representations and projections of the concept "unlimited," inasmuch as they have been traditionally considered free of human imperfection and flaws, a hybrid of humans and machines carries symbolic meaning that now constitutes a perennial vision. Because of this seduction of the mind, if a superior post-human being emerges, a critical line will be crossed and the very concept of human nature will disappear. As a matter of fact, the human body will be dismissed as something of accidental significance, as no more than the material residence of computing software. (For example, if a different hardware is more effective, why not modify it?) In other words, this new version of anthropological dualism reduces the body to a mere container for the human mind, neglecting humanity's natural milieu which is rooted in personal otherness. Theorists of transhumanism argue that the self would be instanti-

[2] "Transhumanism" is the idea that humans should transcend their current natural state and limitations through the use of technology—that we should embrace self-directed human evolution.

ated in some physical medium, but not necessarily one that is biologically human—or biological at all.

Yet, this viewpoint disregards the fact that being human is far more than the sum of computed thoughts and processes. Being human inherently involves a sense of continuity, an experience of deep communion, a constant reconstruction of meanings, a struggle for discovering personal truth, and a progress towards self-transcendence, among many other things. Ironically, psychoanalysis as a search for human meaning now seems to be an excellent ally of religion and theology in terms of resisting the technocracy of transhumanism, despite the fact that in the past a mutual hostile predisposition between it and religious faith has been common.

Nove sed non nova

All *Liturgy* by nature has the power or quality of creating. It is productive. Perhaps this is why the Liturgy (and prayer, when it is not just a monologue) is always a surprise. Only when a *space* is opened for God to intercede can the chanting of the same old Cherubic hymn that has been sung countless times in the church (or like Mozart's popular Little Serenade that has been performed thousands of times) feel surprisingly new. Here we experience *nove sed non nova*—the same realities and the same topics of conversation are experienced in a new, different way—reinvigorated by our knowledge of the Purpose in the everlasting *Sabbatical*—the *Eucharist* of the Church. In this we need to trust the dynamics of the faith of the Church. The Eucharistic celebration in our modern times can unlock locked hearts and conceivably speak many foreign and strange languages. The number of languages and ways to express our "surreal" God is infinite and not restricted to one style.

Why, in our time, is every encounter with what is "other," "different," or "new" perceived as threatening in our church circles and congregations? Why have "mediocrity" and poor imitation become the standard? And why do those steeped in mediocrity shape the future of our church life? An innovative religious teacher, a creative iconographer, an enthusiastic priest ... they often have to bow to mediocrity. Why must their unusual style (the fruit of being engrossed in the desire for Christ and changed by his love) be regarded as rival to institutional norms that do not care for personal charisma? Our tragedy lies in accepting such a state of mediocrity that tends to *denigrate* authenticity. "A man who comes to terms with such a self-image—and then projects that image onto God—is a mediocre person that, as a consequence, ends up with a 'mediocre' God. Such a man reduces himself to a diluted, diminished creature, lost in this nothingness unbecoming of a God-like man," warns Bishop Atanasije of Herzegovina.

We lack the *sincerity* of a child's smile, which is the only remedy that can help us remove the masks of superficiality and pretense, and in so doing conquer worlds, present and future. This is a necessary condition for the *sudden* visit of the Spirit, who will pour out on young generations ("and your sons and your daughters shall prophesy," Acts, 2:17) the freedom and genuineness of the *Last Day*.

Young Nicholai Velimirović,
acrylic on canvas, 2022, Bishop Maxim

As a young theologian, Nicholai bequeathed a singular theological legacy that exceeded the established perceptions of his time. His awareness of the need for "inculturation"—that is, for preaching and witnessing the Gospel in ways which meet the cultural needs of the people—led him to the creation of highly exemplary and contemporary works, significant even in our postmodern era. His entire life struggle was a process of contextualizing the evangelical message of the Resurrected Christ.

SEEING THE INVISIBLE

Living the *present* moment while waiting for the future to unfold is an *ideal* opportunity to value life for what it is. In the 1938 metatheatrical play *Our Town,* by American novelist and playwright Thornton Wilder, an extremely interesting dialogue between Emily, one of the characters, and the stage manager takes place. Emily returns to earth to relive one day, her twelfth birthday. She watches with joy at being able to see her parents and some of the people of her childhood. Her joy, however, quickly turns to sorrow when she realizes how little people appreciate the simple joys of life. The memory proves too painful for her, and she turns toward the stage manager and asks: "Do any human beings ever realize life while they live it, every, every minute?" At first, he responds, "No," but after a moment he adds, "saints and poets, maybe—they do some."

Several years ago in Constantinople, after the ordination of Metropolitan Maximos of Sylivria, a discussion ensued at the table about the relationship between the past and the future. One of the participants was the theologian Fr. Paul McPartlan. He stated that our generation tends to neglect the importance of the present moment. "Who cares about the *sacredness* of the *now*?" asked this Roman Catholic priest (who, incidentally, wrote a compelling comparative study in theology on arguably the most influential theologians of the twentieth century, John Zizioulas and Henri de Lubac). Indeed, how are we to cultivate the sacredness of *each* moment without postponing the Eschata? The intention, or the will, to make life a lasting "today," still a long way from realization (since we are on the road to the true *now*), is the most fundamental trait of Christian faith and worship. For we do not look for the Kingdom by contemplating it, but by valiantly fighting for it. And the will implies freedom (self-determination) and drama (creating in history).

Living the sacredness of the *present* moment (while awaiting confirmation of it by some future event, "holding on to heaven while walking the earth," as one Serbian poet said) opens an opportunity to perceive many events otherwise invisible to the naked eye. In fact, the biggest part of the *reality* is neither visible nor accessible to us. And by this, I do not just mean the cosmic expanses of our universe. Remember the awe when you first saw footage of life from the bottom of the ocean, that largest habitat on the planet that we know the least about. Creatures that come in astounding variety of sometimes bizarre shapes, vibrant colors, and the underwater scenery ... it takes one's breath away! As the light energy travels through the water, the molecules in the water scatter and absorb it. At great depths, light is so scattered that there is nothing left to detect visually, and in depths below 1000 meters there is an "aphotic" zone where there is no light at all. So, how is it even possible that in the deepest darkness, which is characteristic of the deep-sea environment, there exists the greatest and the most vibrant ecosystem full of colors and life, consisting of everything from jellyfish to big tuna? Organisms in this zone have many strategies for *camouflage* in order to find food, they blend in with their surroundings to avoid becoming prey. Many creatures that live at the bottom of the ocean (including corals) are colored in shades of red, and some of them produce their own light called *bioluminescence.* Their shapes and colors are the most beautiful sight to see. Paradoxically, way down there at the bottom of the ocean, the darkest darkness and its dwellers that display an astonishing array of vibrant colors exist together. What does that tell us?

A monk's habit does not make the monk

We will probably see a real picture (icon, image, mien) of all the different beings and personalities around us—who are sometimes covered with thicker and at other times thinner veils—in their marvelous beauty only when the lively hues of paradise become part of our permanent setting. In the meantime, the appearances and costumes that we use to cover up often serve as an image of our future look, sometimes as a shelter, sometimes as a camouflage. When I was preparing to leave for Greece to study, one of my professors gave me interesting advice: "When you return from your studies, my dear colleague, please do not show up wearing a long beard and a habit with wide sleeves." I did not understand it at the time, but many years later I realized that this professor felt not so much that other people's customs do not fit into the Serbian cultural space, but, more importantly, that outward appearance does not say much about the inner man. "L'habit ne fait pas le moine" ("A monk's habit does not a monk make"), says a French proverb, probably originating from an historical event when François Grimaldi and his companions captured the fortress of Monaco by disguising themselves as Franciscan monks.

The monks of Mount Athos have a wide variety of "styles" of clothing and each hat is differently cut, which is the upshot (as someone suggested to me) of authenticity and vibrancy that radiates from within. Virtue has nothing to do with outward appearances or a dress code. But, apart from attire, one might just as easily "put on" rhetorical displays, philosophical sophisms, stylistic arabesques, or theological truisms, in order to overpower the interlocutor or even deceive the entire church. Behind these phenomena lies the vice of self-love: "you are like whitewashed tombs, which outwardly indeed appear lovely, but within are filled with the bones of the dead and with all uncleanliness. Thus you also outwardly indeed appear upright, but within you are full of dissimulation and lawlessness" (Matthew 23:28-27). Christ, however, liberates us from idolatrous monologue of a Christian solipsist and takes us to a different world. That which is *different* is that grain of salt that prevents us from becoming insipid.

The Liturgy itself, as a celebration of the *ever-new* Pascha, suffers neither the principle of *una faccia, una razza*, nor automatism. (On the eve of one pan-Orthodox service in America, hierarchs and priests from various jurisdictions asked a bishop "what color of vestments to wear," so everything would be "uniform." The bishop intentionally told each of them a different color. The Liturgy was thus suffused with colors, the sight resembling the one from the ocean floor). To begin with, let us not be guided solely by *habit*. Sometimes habits perpetuate mistakes and create a mentality that labels everything as a "God-given practice," or create a psychological phenomenon known as *automatism*. If I want to get to know a person—that is, a person as *another identity*—then I should not limit my judgment to what is visible, but ought to try to somehow "see" what cannot be seen with a naked eye. Admittedly, we cannot know the *essence* of anything (cf. 1 Cor. 2:11). Thus, St. Gregory the Theologian (*Oration* 29) points out that not only God, but even the nature of creation, is far *beyond* the grasp of reason. Nevertheless, while we cannot know the essence of anything, we are still able to see *how* something exists. This means that various aspects of the Other (and other), that are not being revealed to us, have yet to be learned. In that sense, whenever I look at my neighbor I also take into consideration what is not visible to eye. In a *personal* encounter, one is always revealed more than our vision can discern because the truth about the encounter is *above* nature. *Reality* is not a reliable base for knowledge—the sceptics were right about that.

When the saints go marching in

Similarly, certain "eccentrics" (in the language of Church, clairvoyants, fools for Christ's sake) of our time are capable of setting standards that come into practice only after a long time has passed. For example, the 2004 encyclical of the Synod of the Greek Church—according to which, based on liturgical sources, priests are encouraged to read aloud all the prayers of the Liturgy—has replaced the encyclical from 1956. And what was the background of that first encyclical? Its purpose was to "condemn" Dionysius, the renowned Metropolitan of Kozani (in central Greece) for having dared to read the liturgical prayers *aloud*. Interestingly, this first encyclical provided no theological argument but merely referred to the need to preserve "*uniformity*." Dionysius of Kozani was therefore considered an exception, the "black sheep" of Hellas, because the ecclesiastical *status quo* could not *see* as deep and far as he could. It took 50 years for the *entire* church hierarchy to conform to a truth carried by a single hierarch.

Applied to our ecclesiastical reality, there are so many effective ways of communication around us that we are *not even aware of.* There are opportunities in all fields: educational, parochial, episcopal and... *synodal*! Why should Orthodox Church leaders not hold occasional teleconferences, or why not start the practice of convening *ad hoc* regional synods? Imagine such news one day: "the synods of the Serbian, Bulgarian, Romanian and Greek Churches met to discuss *burning* issues in the Balkans: the threat to a sanctity of personality, the migrant crisis, the heresy of ethnophyletism," etc. This is especially relevant given that the great jubilee is approaching in 2025, the 1700th anniversary of the First Ecumenical Council of Nicaea (325), since the 4th century showed a greater level of communication among bishops than the beginning of the third millennium.

And have you heard about Bishop Nicholai's hat? Behind a seemingly secular suit a saint of our time can hide. I do not know if it was a style of the time, or something else, but in America during that period such saintly characters as Mardarije of Libertyville and Nicholai of Zhicha[1] were seen dressed up in suits and hats. Those were times as difficult and complex as ours. But in situations when they had to meet with people from *other* (different) walks of life, they occasionally wore suits, coats and ... hats. I am afraid that

[1] Saint Nicholai of Ohrid and Zhicha (1880–1956) has been called the "New Chrysostom" for his theological depth and golden-tongued eloquence. St. Mardarije of Libertyville and Chicago, missionary and first Serbian bishop in America (1935). He served with self-sacrificial energy despite being gravely ill.

we Christians, and those of higher hierarchical rank, are often not ready to realize that the gaze of the Other makes us also more visible to ourselves. When we are "alone" in the modus of pure *diocesan* "isolation" then we act as if there were no others; in front of us is only the horizon on which our neighbors appear and disappear. When others observe us, we can get to know ourselves better. The leitmotif of church hermeneutics is that knowledge—as well as being—is not static. Therefore, it is not enough to say that some truth is "ontological" (simply to emphasize its importance), since there are many different ontologies. We are not interested in the ontology that deals with reality *as such*, but in the "neverlandish" type of ontology which requires that our reality is being acknowledged by the *other* person. This goes beyond the illusion of the idolatrous self-sufficiency of the world. The true ecclesiastical *modus* is the one that indiscriminately supports us in our call to share the mind of Christ, which liberates us from the autonomy of "reason" and leads to true dialogue in the Church.

I believe we all dream of a Church where we would begin *anew* (based on the Pauline vision of holiness) to envision humanity as a community of diversity—where we all share charisma, ascetic endeavors, ministries ... and rejoice that there is such diversity in the types of ministries—led by a local bishop "at the divine council" (Ps. 81:1). Living in this vision all of us, in our distinct positions, would begin the *communal, humble yet elated* service to the whole society. The song "*When the saints go marching in*" would become everyone's apocalyptic ode that would place all of the "royal priesthood" into service to the Lamb! And we might even sing that song led by Louis Armstrong himself and his orchestra from 1938. Indeed, we cannot progress (come out of the present crisis) if we do not have the *desire* to do so, which can only stem from our admiration for Christ. Gregory the Theologian describes that desire in the following way: "...and as an object of wonder to become more an object of desire, and, by being desired to purify, and by purifying to make us *like God*, so that, when we have thus become like Himself, God may, to use a bold expression, hold converse with us as gods, *being united to us*, and that perhaps to the same extent as He already knows those who are *known* to Him." (*Oration* 38). Let his words be a prayer that may lead to a change of heart in us sinners.

Young Georges Florovsky *Leaving Odessa and Heading to the West*, acrylic on canvas, 2022, Bishop Maxim

Young Florovsky, with an expressive face, is immersed in his thoughts, while on the horizon are discerned his hometown Odessa in flames of a then distant war, Paris and New York. The painting offers an humanitarian aspect of Florovsky's theology.

THE WAY AND CHINESE CHRISTIANITY

Caravaggio's *The Calling of Saint Matthew* (c. 1600) depicts the moment at which Christ calls upon Levi to follow him and become the apostle Matthew. In the painting Christ points to Levi the tax-collector, who is seated at a table with four other people. Surprised by the intrusion, Levi draws back with an expression of astonishment on his face. In His unparalleled, divine way, Christ summons Matthew and this moment inspires a man to follow Him (cf. Matthew 9:9). That summoning of the Apostle and Levi's gaze excite awe. Undoubtedly, all four Gospels show that from the moment of Christ's calling and one's conversion life assumes a new dimension for His followers. To a woman who had been suffering a discharge of blood, a single touch was enough to transform her long suffering into the blessing of a *new* life, life as a perpetual miracle. This does not mean that after being converted or healed we are to keep Christ to ourselves.

In a number of Gospel passages we find phrases such as "they were astounded," "they marvelled," and "they were astonished" (Matthew 7:28; 9:33; 12:23; 13:54). In Mark this sense is heightened even more: "And immediately they were astonished, very greatly astonished." (5:42). True knowledge, and love for hypostatic wisdom, always begins in wonder. Socrates, in Plato's *Theaetetus,* says that *wonder* (θαυμάζειν) is the feeling of a philosopher, and that philosophy begins in wonder (an echo of this passage can be found in Aristotle's *Metaphysics*: "It is wonder, admiration, that led the first philosophers to philosophy," and still does).

It is said that today's generation is characterized by a certain amount of indifference to life. Has this also become true of the Church environment? Something similar happened in the time of Symeon the New Theologian: during that period of the Byzantine Empire when everything flourished in the political, cultural and other fields, the astonishing stream of the living faith somehow sunk into the ruts of formalism. And Symeon reacted, reminding his contemporaries that the reality of the "new creation" in Christ (2 Corinthians 5:17) is a matter of present, not past concern. "This is what is accomplished and takes place daily in the true faithful and chosen ones. While yet in the body, as we have often said, they become *conscious* partakers, in part, of these things" (*Fifth Ethical Discourse*). This theologian—at first ironically called the "new theologian" by his opponents—integrated into the Church's tradition the Christ-centered and God-inspired ethos of knowledge and union with God in love, and introduced a dimension of *wonder* and *visions.*

As I meander the streets of Nanjing, capital of China's eastern Jiangsu province, and watch in wonder the faces of thousands of people, I timidly ask the Lord,

"When will a nation of over one billion people receive a *miracle* like the one that happened at the time of Cyril and Methodius?" At the same time, I am careful not to stare at anyone for too long because in Asian countries it is considered impolite to look directly at people. Orthodox Korean iconographers, for instance, portray the saints with their eyes averted. The traditions of Confucianism, Taoism and Buddhism have left a collective and lasting impression on Chinese culture, which is almost 5000 years old. The eyes of a beholder must not *outstep* the boundaries of social norms, for the eye is the chief organ necessary for *aesthetic* knowledge. Traditional Chinese virtues, such as harmony, charity, righteousness, kindness, honesty, loyalty and friendly affection, are woven into their culture. This aretological connection is reflected in the eyes of Chinese men and women which convey the innermost pulsations of the soul, while other facial characteristics naturally reflect aspects dependent on the local *ethos*. For the Chinese, the correlation and collaboration of eyes with an outward expression (individual and collective sensibility) is indissoluble and almost absolute. I think that narrow and slanted Asian eyes, although they are just one of the facial characteristics (including the mouth, nose, forehead, chin and cheeks), emit quite a different energy. The face truly reflects not just the society we live in, but the entire cosmos. To a European, the Asian face appears *prima facie* expressionless, inscrutable. But with a little effort, while drinking tea with them, he will discover an extraordinary psychological, existential expression on it.

In order to understand (and evangelize) China, I think it is important to study physiognomy, especially the face, for it can help us see the "hidden man of the heart"—a bringing outward, an ex-pressing, of an internal reality that overflows with emotion. It is a deep existential state that the face communicates, thus taking a missionary to another plane, to some other level. The phenomenon of the facial expressions of the Chinese is altogether different from the Japanese. Although the Chinese face is a seemingly stylized face, it gives you a very strong expression, so dynamic that no Hollywood makeup artist can conjure it. The Chinese smile is discreet, *hesychastic*, and because of that, it makes the face radiant. Physiognomy and psychology reveal the face here as a *gift of God*, and this is the most interesting aspect of Chinese social psychology. Abstract and untouchable, the face is the finest "standard" by which, some would say, the social relations in China are regulated.

A face as an image of the cosmos

Consequently, I carefully observed the people in the streets of Nanjing in an attempt to penetrate into the profound mystery of that nation, gathering, through eyes, a multitude of insights about this ancient civilization. (Of course, Chinese youth are also staring at their phones as they walk the streets.) In those moments of contemplating the evangelization of this people, I was probably oblivious to the fact that I, being a foreigner, could not prevent my inner world from showing on *my* face. Sometimes we refer to the "inculturation" of the Gospel (and concern for Christian unity) as a *noetic* concept—but for Chinese Christians, *evangelization* has been a matter of life and death (as was revealed during the anti-colonial Boxer Uprising, 1899-1901).

"Hindrances" that those people face need not be mentioned if we bear in mind the political milieu and the vastness of this country of the Himalayas, the Gobi Desert, the Yangtze River and the "Silk Road," the Yellow Sea, the Great Wall, with lowlands and mountainous areas (which make up about two-thirds of China's total territory).

In the 7th century, Assyrian Christians lived in this region. The Chinese called their teaching the "religion of light," until Assyrian Christianity disappeared in religious persecutions of later centuries. There were also the Franciscan missionaries, followed by the Jesuits, and then the Orthodox, some of whom were declared martyrs. The first Protestant missionaries from the early 19th century endeavored to translate the Scriptures into Chinese (the Bible was fully translated only a hundred years ago) even though their presence was associated with Western colonialism, and the tragedy of opium addiction. Their search for an autonomous Chinese Christianity, and the sufferings they endured in that mission should incite respect rather than condemnation.

In his book *Russian Missions: A Historical Sketch*, Fr. Georges Florovsky wrote about China as "in general a very difficult country and unfavorable for missionary work." He emphasized that every missionary "must have a great philological gift and sensitiveness, a loving and a lively sense of the tongue; a desire and power to penetrate into a foreign soul and understand it; that is to say, one ought, in a certain sense, to have the faculty of sympathetic reincarnation." While a delightful Chinese girl writes her name in my notebook (all the while scolding her mother—in a loving voice—for giving her that name), I realize that the Chinese alphabet is not really an alphabet at all, but an artistic calligraphy. By the way, the Russian Orthodox mission had its beginnings in Beijing in the early 18th century. It was started by the Russian prisoners of war who settled there and who also "gathered information." This missionary effort had no broader implications, for although much had been done in the field of translation, the mission never experienced significant growth. Obviously, a true encounter never occurred.

"Whom you worship not knowing, Him I proclaim to you"

The American hieromonk Seraphim Rose attempted such an encounter by exploring the connection between the Tao and Christ. His efforts alone indicate that the Church, as a relational reality, has continuously been looking for *new* methods throughout her history. She is not a petrified entity that is passed on from one generation to another as an archaeological treasure. Rose's successor, Abbot Damascene of the St. Herman of Alaska Monastery in Platina, California, ventured to consider the ancient book of Chinese philosophy, the *Tao Te Ching* (credited to the sixth-century BC sage Lao Tzu), in the light of Christian revelation, seeing Lao's *Tao* as the harbinger of Christ and the wise Lao Tzu as a prophet. Damascene's book, *Christ the Eternal Tao,* is an antidote to Western obsession with Eastern religions—yet another symptom of the shallowness of modern culture.

Thales, the first among the Greek philosophers, lived around the 6th century BC, which made him a contemporary of Confucius in China and Buddha in India. Heraclitus was born in the mid-6th century BC and is known for his teaching about the *logos* as the universal principle of philosophy and existence (i.e., the unity of the world, for the logos maintains the total balance of the cosmos at all times). By chance, or not, the Chinese philosopher Lao Tzu lived at the same time as Heraclitus and also wrote about the same universal principle of order. He said, "I do not know its name. If I am forced to give it a name, I call it Tao (*Way*), and I name it as supreme." He also proffered the advice to "Use your own light and return to the source of light." Thus, "Tao" is to Chinese philosophy what "Logos" is to Greek philosophy. While the former was regarded as a transpersonal reality and the latter as the principle of life, five centuries later the Logos came as the Truth personified.

Six centuries after Heraclitus and Lao Tzu, the Holy Apostle and Evangelist John the Theologian lived on the Greek island of Patmos. There, in exile in an island cave, the Son of Thunder dictated to his disciple Prochoros what came to him from God by direct revelation. "In the origin there was the Logos, and the Logos was present with GOD, and the Logos was God." And thus the Tao becomes *flesh* that, perhaps in the future, may rid the Chinese religion of mysticism and make it *incarnate* (although the Chinese believe in reincarnation, they are still terribly afraid of death). To depart from the Tao (to stray from the Path) means to miss the mark, *hamartia*. The Chinese Way, once the natural (protological) introversion has been overcome, could serve as a magnificent bridge to Christianity.

As I depart from this mysterious country, I pray that the Lord will multiply His ministers in all the corners of the earth! In the distance can be heard the echo of the prologue to John's Gospel in the spirit of the Chinese idiom, as interpreted by the God-seeker Seraphim Rose: "In the origin there was the *Tao* (Way), and the *Tao* was present with God, and the *Tao* was God ... In Him was life, and this light was the life of men ..."

Post scriptum. In our culture little is known that since the first translations of the prologue of John's Gospel (John 1: 1) into Chinese, most of them use the word "tao" or "dao" for "logos." In the Russian Church, that translation solution was accepted without any problems. Thus, a book entitled *V načale bylo Dao* (*In the beginning there was the Tao*) was written by Seraphim Petrovski, head of the Center for the Far East at the Moscow Spiritual Academy, and published by the Kruticki Courtyard of the Moscow Patriarchate in 2007. The analogy (but not the identification) of the logos-tao has its basis in the fact that Christ is the hypostatic *Way* (cf. Jn 14: 5-6).

***A Pensive William Shakespeare*,**
acrylic on canvas, 2022, Bishop Maxim

An intense portrait, revealing a nice posture, and highlighting the face—weighty, thinking, with a discrete smile. The paper he reads is a bit crumpled, perhaps a little stained. On paper, the imprints of lived time bring to the portrait the life of inanimate time. His garment, with its horizontal strokes, intimates a writer who meditates and walks a little bent over-an intellectual who writes the history of the spirit, and does not need uniforms, medals, and crowns. The background discreetly but expressively reveals the inner spiritual storms that Shakespeare lived while fighting with the spirits.

CULTURE, POLITICS AND THE CONSOLATION OF THEOLOGY

As the unpleasant truth becomes more and more apparent, not even the latest *condition humaine* can tarnish it. While a group of young Prizren seminarians (from Serbia's Kosovo and Metohia) sings the hymn circling around the Notre Dame, like children circling around their mother, I am searching (*à la recherche*) for a pen to capture those sacred moments which will soon only be memories. The hymn to the Virgin Mary, in any harmonic system, tonality or scale, is never monotonous.

While not losing sight of their own heritage (or, for a moment at least ... setting aside national "stories about identity" as too difficult a theme), those young seminarians from Kosovo and Metohija seek to build their character by taking a course about French tradition and culture. It is presented to them by the best instructor possible, Mr. Ljuba Mihailović, whose life story is worthy of a book, or a film, in the style of his grandfather Svetozar Botorić, the first film producer in the Balkans. Ljuba recommends to them the 1966 black-and-white film *Is Paris Burning?*—one of the best war films about French resistance—in which the Notre Dame and the surrounding area eventually appear in color (an ending that Tarkovsky also liked). Today, he is showing the best of Paris to Prizren theologians (Paris is not all about elegance and virtue, and the eye of a beholder sees not *only* beauty).

Shakespeare knows me

There is something "stereotypical" about the lives of many who are ranked among the great minds of history. Only a few were popular during their time. The great Photius of Constantinople (820-893) spent the last years of his life in exile. Mozart was celebrated only after his death. Van Gogh only managed to sell one canvas in his lifetime. We all remember Tesla's fate in New York or Bishop Nicholai's in Pennsylvania. Prophets are rarely accepted by their generation, and yet their eventual recognition comes in the form of a consolation that offers some refreshment to a tired humanity. "Bach is so great, as a being almost beyond humanity, and at the same time his music affords us the greatest consolation," said the French author and poet Christian Bobin. Perhaps the words that Ben Johnson addressed to Shakespeare can be applied to all of the greats: "He was not just for his generation, but for all generations." Admittedly, Shakespeare (1564-1616) was somewhat respected during life, though we have no contemporary physical description of his appearance, nor is there any indication that he had his portrait made. Some condemned him for mixing tragic and comic elements. It was not until the 18th century that critics began to appreciate his genius, while the modernist revolution in art during the early 20th century classified his work as avant-garde.

No one has expanded the dramatic potential of character, plot, language and genre like Shakespeare. The modern man can understand the greatness of Shakespeare's opus by comparing it to Martin's fantasy book, *Game of Thrones*. Actress Naomi Watts claims that George Martin achieved success similar to Shakespeare's. William's plays, written in the late 16th and early 17th centuries for a small repertory theatre, are now performed around the globe. Shakespeare did not apply his radiant spiritual insights to esoteric or distant objects, but to human beings with their broad range of emotions and conflicts. That is why St. Nicholai of Zhicha said: "I do not know Shakespeare. Even I cannot know him. But *he knows me*; he described me, he painted all the secrets of my soul in such a way that in reading him I am finding myself in him."

Do the examples I have mentioned signify that *Omega* preestablishes *Alpha* (and, therefore, the rest of the letters of the alphabet)? Whatever you believe on the subject, the fact remains that only the next generation is able to *evaluate* and confirm some truths passed from the previous generation. When Joseph's brothers—who had previously sold him into slavery—began to apologize to him as they met in Egypt, he told them: *"And now do not be distressed or angry with yourselves because you sold me here, for God sent me before you to preserve life."* (Gen. 45:5). The righteous

Joseph presented this irrefutable truth from the tragic past in a completely different, positive light, thereby relieving his brothers of their unbearable torment. That is why joy is a characteristic of the age to come, because a smile of relief will wipe away sorrow and all tears. Maybe that is why the Nigerian name for God is "Father of Laughter"! In any case, we can speak *de consolatione theologiae* (on the consolation of theology, its meaning and role) only when we acknowledge that God is both the Alpha and Omega at the same time, continually—not Alpha today and then Omega tomorrow.

We are beginning to resemble modern Frenchmen. Namely, recent French history textbooks describe France's history through the prism of world history, so much of what is truly French is not being taught today. Macron, certain in his assessment that French society has become multicultural, has ventured to say that French culture no longer exists. This leader has forgotten what attracts millions of visitors a year to come to his country from all over the world. Also, thanks to bad history being taught in French schools, their politicians know very little about other countries. Macron is sceptical of the new expansion of the European Union in a situation where the twenty-eight members cannot reach consensus.

In his book, *The New Silk Roads*, described by some as a brilliant guide to *terra incognita*, Peter Frankopan explains some of the twists and turns in the world's center of gravity. It reminds us of the importance of the Far and Middle East for the balance of world relations and hence the future of humanity. I believe books like this help us to better understand cultural complexity. Undoubtedly, the more complex the world, the less comprehensible it becomes for the general public. For example, during the Cold War, personal opinions and the finding of solutions were both contained within the East-West dilemma. This dilemma also hinders today's discourse; the individual feels insecure because he cannot understand exactly what is happening around him, and neither secular nor spiritual institutions are helping. That is why *conspiracy theories* are flourishing.

St. Photius and Machiavelli

The less social knowledge, the more authoritarian and alienated state power grows. Recent political developments in Turkey can serve as a warning to autocrats in the world. Whenever we see a ruler's political support dwindle, it might be a good moment to remind ourselves not only how *fickle* is the *obedience* of the masses (i.e., obedience without personal responsibility), but also that at one time the Patriarch of Constantinople gave counsel to the monarch. Around the year 865, Saint Photius the Great wrote the letter to *Khan Boris-Michael of Bulgaria* (Ὁ Ἡγεμών, hegemon, ruler, prince). The letter contains, among other particulars, moral and political lessons of wider significance. Photius did not have in mind some prosaic goal since, as will be seen, the main purpose of a "ruler" or a statesman is much deeper and more lasting.

According to St. Photius, a ruler should rise above strife between parties and address the problems of his subjects with compassion and understanding. There is no excuse for a ruler who commits injustice, nor are there mitigating circumstances. (Whereas a poor man can at least have an excuse for unjust behavior because of his poverty.) A ruler who acts contrary to virtue makes a threefold mistake: he harms himself, antagonizes those around him, and blasphemes against God who gave him the throne. The ruler can be the judge of others only if he himself conscientiously accounts for his actions and tries to correct his mistakes. It is commendable if he also resolutely unmasks injustice by employing prudence and righteousness. A reasonable ruler should avoid over-promising and not deviate from the given task, for he will deserve condemnation if he does not fulfill it. Firm in his positions, he needs to carefully choose words and master his tongue. Likewise, ministers should be people rich in virtue, because corrupt politicians will cast a shadow over him as well. The ruler should make sure that the traditions and customs of his native country are not obliterated. Introducing innovations in an invasive way will cause anxiety and confusion and will aggravate people.

There is no statesman today with qualities that fit the model of an exemplary ruler. Although idealistic, this does not mean Photius' ruler should not be a model for imitation to leaders of the present age. The advice of Patriarch Photius to the Bulgarian ruler is inspired by the Hellenic-Christian spirit and is an antipode to the utilitarian and amoral understanding of power, as expressed in Nicholas Machiavelli's famous book *The Prince* and applied both in the West and later in the East. Certainly, models and archetypes from the past should not be the only standard by which we measure the present human condition. "The talent to follow the path of our ancestors is not enough to improve today's world," said an emperor of one region in southeast China. Can this text of Photius the Great serve as a boundary that separates the ancient Hellenic from the prevailing understanding of realpolitik today? In any case, it shows that a healthy political awareness should also be built on other, non-political elements. It is based on the way in which a free person (of any age) is brought up and educated in order to represent a part of a communal personality. In such circumstances, a citizen with spiritual freedom thinks creatively, not defensively. His decisions about the future are ideally based on a realistic picture of the intricate nuances of today's world.

A very different type of Polis

Whatever way we look at it, Photius' letter to the Bulgarian archon Michael—as a real-life counterpart to Machiavelli's *Prince*—can serve (less as an instruction manual and more as a warning) contemporary church leaders in helping them to understand that their role is to remind rulers of their *main* purpose. Today, when the relationship between state and church have become widely talked about, it might be worth recalling the principle of "a free church in a free state" as a measure for mutual interaction. This calls for a *prophetic* attitude towards any government, especially today when the state system has made the Church irrelevant. It is, however, not only in the interest of the state that the role of Church continues to be marginalized and made obsolete, but is also in the interest of some church leaders. Hence the price any bishop pays for reminding politicians that they work for the people will be dear. Saint Photius successfully advised the Bulgarian ruler, but had no luck with Byzantine emperors. After the death of Emperor Basil, his son Leo became emperor. In 886 Leo deposed an aged Photius from the patriarchal throne and sent him into exile. He spent the last five (or six) years of his life in a deserted monastery near Constantinople. "And in fact, all who seek to live a godly life in Christ Jesus will be persecuted," (2 Timothy 3:12). The Church, that icon of the Kingdom of God on earth, has often proved powerless in history. Yet when she is gathered "on the Lord's day" (Rev. 1:10), she will see "a new heaven and a new earth" (21:1). As Photius' case shows, the role of the Church is not to improve living conditions by offering ready-made solutions for better economic or political systems (or, for that matter, methods for psychosomatic *well-being*). If she truly testifies that Christ has conquered death and brought Eternal Life, then she can also serve society by offering hope, because she is a very different type of *polis*, "a city set upon the hill" (Matthew 5:14).

The "Patron Saint of Reviewers," as Henry Chadwick called St. Photius, opens the rooms of his *Library* (his beautiful book "Miriobiblos" or "Library") to us and encourages us to read and learn from classical (ancient and Christian) writers. At the same time, his *Prince* can open to our state and church diplomats an additional eye (διπλό-μάτι, double-eye), and, in so doing, make them see more clearly both the true spiritual *telos* and the national *character*, beyond *momentary* (geo)political interests.

Elder Sophrony of Essex,
acrylic on canvas, 2022, Bishop Maxim

According to St. Sophrony, the quintessence of the monk's calling is not escape from the world, but continuous residence "in God."

A FLEXIBLE, DIVINE GRACE

The counsels of a twentieth-century spiritual father to modern man can be summed up in three core philosophies—do not despair, do not be sentimental, and do not force yourself to do anything. These axioms provide guidance and keys to growth because they lead one to the discovery of the authentic person through a triune experience of enthrallment, realism and freedom (which are the antipodes to the three previously mentioned spiritual conditions).

Only when we break away from established tastes or puritanism can we start gaining a different kind of knowledge and aesthetics. For example, when we do not reject that which is other or different (in any way); when we think to ourselves during a musical performance that it does not matter that the pianist played a wrong note; when we are not annoyed that a priest used the wrong exclamation at the end of a litany; when we are glad that we can forgive ourselves and others for abandoning a "principle"; and when we are not overly troubled when our instincts betray us. True contemplation and true perception of beauty come only when selfish interests are abandoned. Aesthetic insight cannot know what may lay ahead on this creative journey. Stephen Zweig felt this beautifully when he wrote *The Mystery of Artistic Creation*—so much so, he noted, that "the only thing we can do is to reconstruct this act once it has taken place and even then it is possible to do so only to a certain extent." Of course, one should not become enamored with human achievements or the glory and triumph of civilization, especially because "the time has been made short... and those who make use of the cosmos might be like those who do not exploit it; for the shape (τὸ σχῆμα, *form*) of the cosmos is passing away" (1 Cor. 7:29, 31).

What is stopping us from experiencing a familiar passage for the Bible, an intelligent theological or philosophical text, or a remarkable musical oeuvre in a way that can take us to new and unexplored territories? Is it because of our reprobate mind? Or numbed senses? Both, together with our attachment to this world and the things of the world, play an equal role. Our own pretenses and self-deception also impede us. We often use elaborate tricks to show that we are able to do more than we can or know how to. We want to prove that the other person is wrong, so we develop sophisticated arguments. We strive so hard to persuade others of our love that we suffocate them. We are all too ready to rebuke the church reader for intoning a litany normally intoned by a deacon, or to admonish the priest who, in a makeshift church in a cowboy saloon somewhere in Texas, had nowhere else to place the Eucharistic gifts but on the piano. These are examples of constraints imposed by an egoistic desire to make others happy by forcing our vision of life on them, instead of extracting the best from what life has to offer. We are not ready to commend the wonderful ability of others to shed light on the most complex theological truths/concepts to people either inside or outside the Church. We are envious because we are not free and do not love. Underneath our polished exterior there hides no spirit of an apostolic journey of discovery and adventure in the Holy Spirit.

If, while continuing our ascetic practices nonetheless, we give up our rigid imperatives, we might still be strengthened in the knowledge of the "gift." The graceful intrusion into this side of heaven through a fissure in the sky renders a harsh reality transparent to perception, thereby providing us a glimpse of the Creator and His love. That is the moment when we acknowledge to God that He is unrelentingly merciful. A barely literate Russian peasant and ardent ascetic named Silouan prayed long and with tearful cries, "Lord have mercy on me!" He felt as if God had forsaken him. His disciple Sophrony Sakharov, a famous ascetic, esthete and teacher of the principle of "hypostatic prayer," in a modern hagiographic piece describes how Silouan, after many months of prayer whereby his strength was exhausted, lost heart and cried out, "You are implacable!"

> When, at these words something foundered in his soul, grown weak from despair, he suddenly beheld the living Christ in the Divine light. His heart and body were filled with fire of such force that had the

> vision continued for another instant, he would have died. Afterwards he was never to forget the inexpressibly gentle, infinitely loving, joyous gaze of Christ full of peace; and during the long years of his life that were to follow he tirelessly bore witness that God is love, love immeasurable, love incomprehensible.

This happened in the church, during the vespers service. In this description, we do not encounter a typical "synergy." Seeking the Lord should not be misconstrued to imply the quest for some instant gratification that employs a reciprocal relation (I do something then you do something in return, and so on). On the contrary, there is an "inherent antinomy in true ascesis," as Fr. Georges Florovsky lucidly remarked, since the grain of wheat cannot bear fruit unless it dies (cf. John 12:24). Elder Sophrony of Essex, with his highly-refined psychological sense and an outstanding skill of portraying people comparable to Father Justin's of Ćelije, depicts a monk who experienced the ineffable sweetness of divine love (as well as demonic assaults), and who in his search for God did not allow despair to rule his heart (keep your mind in hell, but know you are not forsaken by God). This saving message is a covenant for our generation and generations to come.

Censorship, fear, and a forgery

Bearing this in mind, it seems extremely naive and pathetic that the intention of some is to suppress the profusion of theological viewpoints. And our era is unique in this respect. At one time, the young hieromonk Nicholai Velimirović enthusiastically believed in the idea of pan-humanism and the concept of "All-man," he admired some "Hindu ideas," but there existed no official "censors" appointed to sanction him (either by name-calling or denying him any blessing). It is interesting that, at the time, no one was so shortsighted as to insist on the problematic viewpoints of this young theologian because, at that time, such an overly stringent theological censorship did not exist. Rather, the general climate was one that focused on the task-goal (σκοπός) of bringing other peoples and faiths into Christ's fold by the baptism (divinization, transfiguration) of cultural patterns. Nicholai's bold statements and unorthodox digressions were seen rather as a mild paraphony than a slip into heresy. (Nicholai's *paraphony*, was, musically speaking, a sound that was not in harmony with other tones, but still contributed to the melodic unity).

The second instruction is given us by one Herzegovinian bishop through his demystification of sentimentalism. His character is asymmetrical, not only from the outside but also from the inside, but even so he wins us over by his unhypocritical attitude towards everything that exists. Behind his unkempt exterior lies the spirit of freedom and beauty! Ever since I was a child, I have been particularly attracted to thoughtful characters whose gloomy faces hide behind Christ-like grace. Scandinavian writer Fredrik Backman captured the hearts of readers with similar characters in his novel *A Man Called Ove*. This kind of psychological asymmetry has always fascinated me, especially when, only a moment later, an angelic smile of the age to come appears on such a face.

Upon one occasion, during the recent war in Serbia, I worked with other monks in the monastery garden without the slightest inkling that it would someday become a vineyard. The elderly Bishop, who was digging with us, greeted the incoming visitors with gentle rudeness (if one might call it that), not paying them any particular attention. There was not the least bit of saccharine sentimentality in his behavior. This is not the kind of love that holds you back but tells you that you will "go in and will go out" freely (cf. John 10:9). In spite of his abrasiveness, external appearance, and seeming repulsiveness of manner, he unexpectedly radiated only the warmth of love. One visitor later admitted: "He forever won me over when he replied to my flattering compliment with a sobering response that cheap praise would not gain us favor with him." Indeed, when you act spontaneously, you emit a sincerity that makes everything around fall into its proper place.

This leads us to the third instruction left to us by Elder Porphyrios the Kafsokalyvite. It teaches us that grace cannot be received on demand. His advice not to "force ourselves to pray" reminds us of the Savior's words: "Look closely at the lilies in the field—how they grow; they neither labor nor spin," (Matthew 6:28). It is enough for us to seek his kingdom and his justice (cf. Matthew 6:33).

Indeed, there is plenty of hypocrisy behind closed doors. In the provocative novella (now a recent TV series) *Big Little Lies*, writer Liana Moriarty skillfully explores the realities of contemporary parenting, making politics look like a game of chess. It describes the fates of numerous ex-spouses and broken families and artfully reveals what goes on behind closed doors in urban environments.

Unsurpassed dilemmas

Our time is not much different from past epochs, as is shown by some examples from the tenth century. A deeper insight into history reveals that the ideal of the Church is not only about maintaining a continuity of beliefs and standards. Rather, innovations and engagement with significant events also form an essential part of tradition. The Venerable Athanasius the Athonite began the construction of the Great Lavra (a cenobitic monastery) around the year 963, on the spot where his cell originally stood. Many Athonite monks reacted negatively to this, fearing that it would alter the ascetic character of the Holy Mountain. He was criticized for introducing "novelties" (read: "newfangled modernistic ideas"), such as "building expensive temples," "building docks" (read: "paving roads"), "bringing water sources" (read: "infrastructure and technology"), procuring "yokes for oxen" (read: "car fleet"), and "transforming the Holy Mountain into the world!" With this construction, however, St. Athanasius shaped and organized a populous monastery, and created the first cenobitic community that eventually made the Holy Mountain a monastic republic. This happened despite the fact that Athanasius of Athos did not have idyllic relations with public opinion at the time.

Indeed, one cannot please the world and God at the same time. St. Nicholai of Zhicha wrote that "we may please God with truth and justice, whereas it is impossible to please the world in any way, with either truth or lies, with justice or injustice." And in his book *One Hundred Chapters on Love*, this great man adds that this is because God is eternal and unchanging, while the shape of the world is passing and changeable. The latest need of some in the Church to listen more to what people have to say than what the Gospel reveals has closed the doors to productive discussion on the pressing issues of the day. It was not always like that. In 1920, there was talk in the Serbian Church of the possibility of allowing second marriages to younger priests who were left without wives as a result of unforeseen circumstances. The fact that the matter was brought to the Holy Council of Bishops speaks volumes about the charitable attitude of the bishops of that time.

As a continuation of the same discussion from the distant 1920s, let us note that Nicholai, the Bishop of Zhicha, as an envoy of the Serbian Church, was sent to Constantinople to ask the Ecumenical Patriarchate not to ignore the appeal of the Serbian Church regarding the second marriage of priests (as the periodical *Ecclesiastical Truth*, Ἐκκλησιαστικὴ Ἀλήθεια, reported on May 16, 1920). The Synod of this Church took the issue into consideration and later decided that the problem required a more comprehensive analysis and, moreover, a higher decision-making forum (a kind of ecumenical council). The epilogue to this endeavor occurred on December 15, 1920, when the Serbian Church Council formally ruled on the possibility of blessing a second marriage to widowed priests with children. From the ecclesiastical periodicals we learn that there was a vote on this issue, and that Patriarch Dimitri, Gavrilo of Montenegro, Nicholai of Zhicha and a few others voted to approve the marriage of the priests in the spirit of discretion (ecclesiastical economy) and charity. They were defeated by a small majority who preferred to adhere to the letter of the canon and were perhaps more concerned with "what people would say."

The measure of philanthropy is in not having any measure. During a recent tonsure service, when one young monk professed his vows, the bishop of Herzegovina recommended to him to take St. Silouan the Athonite as a model for his life. I believe he wanted that sinful monk never to forget the "inexpressibly gentle, infinitely loving, joyous gaze of Christ full of peace." And that every time he remembers Silouan's cry for help, "You are implacable," a tear should fall down his face.

Elder Porphyrios Kafsokalyvite,
acrylic on canvas, 2021, Bishop Maxim

This Athonite hesychast,who dwelled in the heart of the city understood love as it was revealed by the incarnation of Christ: not as a costless feeling, but as a participation in the suffering of the other. "You should love and experience pain for one you love."

THE PURE WHITE CANVAS

One of the first things you learn in icon-painting class is that there is "repentance." You can always *correct* a mistake (with a few brush strokes or layers of paint). That intervention, in a way, corrects the *past*. But from a human point of view, can anything that has happened in the past be altered, or is it possible (and not less admirable) to wipe out the negative consequences of previous actions?

This so-called *quantum eraser* dilemma in quantum mechanics is expounded by an American theoretical physicist Brian Greene in *The Fabric of the Cosmos*. Noting that "the past cannot be altered in any way by present actions," Greene poses a seemingly "theological" question: "If you cannot change something that has already happened, can you do the next best thing: erase its impact on the present?" Apart from being intriguing, this question is also an example of how cosmology approaches philosophy and even crosses into theology.

Some speak of repentance as the most *realistic* self-knowledge: having seen our failure in the light of the goal God has set for us, we come to understand our position in relation to God, our neighbor, time, space, cosmos ... only then can we see clearly the thick veil settled over our hearts and the blemishes that cover the whiteness of the original image. We can draw a similar analogy about a pure white canvas: when it is well-painted it delights us, when smeared, it baffles us. The first painter who began the practice of leaving areas of the canvas unpainted is not known. Namely, parts of the composition can appear lighter by using a little trick: simply leave desired areas of the canvas unpainted. In that manner, Edgar Degas kept some parts of the white canvas untouched when applying the brush in order to convey a sense of the volume of the dress of his model or the chair on which she was seated. Cézanne, like Degas, left the whiteness of the canvas unpainted to make us more aware of the way brush strokes were used; that is, leaving white areas in order to achieve transparency, and applying colors and gradients to create the effect of depth.

Following that painting method, I once tried to tone down an overly bright yellow color by adding white, but, much to my chagrin, I was unsuccessful. Attempts to *return* to primal purity sometimes feel like a Sisyphean task. But there is hope: if we understand purity not as a return to the *past* (which, as we know, is impossible) but as a glimmer of what is yet to come, then it is possible to obtain purity and shine more clearly than in the beginning ("the one who conquers shall thus be wrapped in white garments," Rev. 3:5; cf. 7:9). The major obstacle to gaining this knowledge is the working of our fallen mind, which prefers to imagine the archetypal rather than the future state of being.

I exist, can somebody hear me?

Repentance is to be understood as a matter of true *existence* which, I believe, we all long for. One graffito on the street of a metropolis simply says, "I exist." What did its author want to say? Did a bishop or priest of that city wonder about its author? How compassionate are we for the suffering of the "wretched" ones around us? The Christian faith cannot be characterized as an infatuation with things spiritual alone. I believe that if we were given a momentary insight into the pain of a tormented humanity we would not stop praying for its salvation. But we are often unaware of the blessing and joy of being *created*, of being a creature of "the One who created and fashioned man." Since we have a Creator, we ought not to feel abandoned. The realization that we are *His* creation makes us grateful. At the same time, if we were for a moment to become aware of the consequences of Christ's resurrection, our life would become a permanent *glorification* of God. An elderly Greek man, armed with such insights, advised a young painter to always paint joyous images.

If the very *presence* of the Church in the world does not give witness to this resurrection-truth with an earnest call to *repentance* and baptism then she is not fulfilling her mission. This is what the current generation, both clergy and laity, should take as a great responsibility before God: to manifest one Church that is not *of* the world but is *in* the world. If the mission of the Church of today is reduced to ideological confrontation with those who think differently, or persecution of those with a different focus (or simply clumsily articulated thoughts), etc., the consequences are detrimental. Our failure to further Christianize society should be the cause of our repentance and search for forgiveness. Every true bishop is called upon to stand up and say at least once: "I ask forgiveness from God and others for not always being up to the task." Does this sound utopian? Maybe. But if it has been done by Christians of bygone centuries, why should ours be an exception!

At the event of the Descent of the Holy Spirit upon the Apostles and the birth of the Church, a double miracle occurred (emphatically emphasized in the second chapter of the Acts): the people present first tasted the *way* of life of the Age to Come (2:1-4). Consequently, they repented (2:38-39) and were baptized (2:41). The Pentecost event shows that when the charismatic presence of the Eschaton is in the world it then awakens to repentance and inclusion (incorporation) into the New Israel, the Church. Therefore, the Church cannot preach a faith that is not concerned with the existential needs of the world. The Church should manifest that she is not opposed to the world. The early community praised God and enjoyed the favor of all the people. Thus, "day by day the Lord added those who were being saved to their company" (2:47).

Can the consequences of past errors be expunged? The topic of repentance brings us closer to the answer. Today's ambiguous attitude toward confession can be overcome if, in the spirit of the aforementioned event, a person comes to realize that the Church accepts a genuine penitent *beforehand*. There is a fascinating example of an act of confession described in an older version of a prayer book. The penitent approaches the priest who places his epitrachelion over the head of the penitent and *first* reads the prayer of forgiveness. Mercy and the understanding of the tragedy of sin is only possible in relation to the One Who comes hereafter. Only by looking to the future can we forgive and receive forgiveness. The future liberates the past and purifies it from its negative aspects.

Freedom as moving forward

It seems that the original meaning of *metanoia*—a word traditionally translated as "repentance" but whose literal meaning is a "change of mind," or "of thinking," or "of intention," or "of the heart"—can become available to us only if we analyze this Greek word. Given its biblical use, the word inevitably points to something "after" or "beyond" (cf. *ta meta ta physika*). If, through real transformation, we go beyond (*meta*) the fallen *nous*, then it *liberates* us from the burden of the past (faults, vices). In any case, the term μετάνοια is most closely connected with the future: "Change your minds (hearts); for the Kingdom of the heavens has drawn near" (Matthew 3:2). *Metanoia* leads to a change of orientation, to finding once again the moral compass that has been lost.

Those who have been enlightened by *metanoia* realize that God does not require any natural *jus talionis*, the law of reward or punishment (e.g. the law of retaliation of Exodus 21:24). By repentance we arrive at the realization that the principle on which the world is founded is *freedom* rather than some "blind" fate. Fr. Georges Florovsky wrote about this in *Metaphysical Prerequisites of Utopianism*: "We speak of this experiment and experience when we contrast the test of faith with a naturalistic experiment, and not of some 'natural theology' that has been removed forever when the Church was instituted." Therefore, in Christianity, white is not simply associated with innocence or "natural" purity. (The idea of painting white paintings was epitomized by the Russian Suprematist Kazimir Malevich, who painted *White on White* in 1918. His theory was that painting should create within its viewers a "pure feeling," which could be achieved through stripping art down to its essence.) Thus, the real history of man is not in the natural unfolding of some innate, natural end, but in *ascetic feats* or, in the words of Florovsky, in the "countless moments of gentle touches of the Divine, in the astounding encounters with God."

I would like to make myself clear now as to avoid being misunderstood later: *l'art pour l'art* (art for art's sake) is a vain endeavor, pure vanity. Thus, I am not juxtaposing art and theology in order to praise art in and of itself, but rather to highlight its expressiveness—its capacity to manifest freedom in remarkable ways. Because of that freedom, art should be associated with the absolute *truth* offered by the Church. In art as in any act of creativity (artists are not just painters or musicians), there is a blessed celebration and sanctification of the world. When the Church has a clear artistic (and social) instinct about the *person*, then others recognize her not as an authoritarian institution but as a spiritual home.

In the twentieth century Greek poetry, where the multi-layered meaning of the word *logos* (λόγος) is often in harmonious *rhythm* with images from life, we discover the primordial lyric. Thus, in a poem of Maria Polidouri we read, "I was born just because you loved me" (μόνο γιατὶ μ 'ἀγάπησες γεννήθηκα), which provides us with a sense of awareness that makes the reverse perspective the prime law of optics. Poetry (and art in general) finds its *raison d'être* only when it speaks very quietly to one reader at a time. This helps us to find our *purpose* in the lives of others (the Greek word ἀνιδιοτέλεια, selflessness, means that one's purpose in life is to serve others, not oneself). Then we come to realize how deeply we have forgotten the *other* person, "I cry because I forgot you, and not because I do not have you," (κλαίω ποὺ σὲ ξέχασα καὶ ὄχι ποὺ δὲν σὲ ἔχω), says the poet Michális Ganás. It is a state in which, according to the verses of Odysseus Elytis, we feel as if we were someone else, and not ourselves, marching on in life (σὰ νά 'μουν ἄλλος κι ὄχι ἐγώ / μὲς στὴ ζωὴ πορεύτηκα). From such experiences the truth emerges that the beauty of our journey does not consist in beautiful landscapes but in how they alter the way we see the world. To put it in a Proustian way, it is not the landscapes that make a journey memorable, but the way we look at them. Or, as Ivo Andrić says of bridges, the most valuable are "those who have seized and held my imagination and my spirit the longest."

We look to the future with our eyes washed by repentance and, by the grace of the Resurrected God-man Who restores us to life every day, we continue to march on through history until the Day of the Lord—the brightest of all days. Repentance thus becomes a *symptom* of the series of unmerited, wondrous encounters with the King of Glory Who will come from on high and sit upon a great, white throne (cf. Rev. 20:11).

The Elder Atanasije *Breaks Through the Darkness of Night with Prayer*, acrylic on canvas, 2021, Bishop Maxim

Divinity emanating through his expression, the broad shoulders and blessed peace of mind of the Elder Atanasije convey the balance between physical and spiritual strength.

Young Maria Skobtsova,
acrylic on canvas, 2021, Bishop Maxim

Now recognized as St. Maria of Paris, this saint is our saint, and we are hers. She fell in love, married, became a mother, and then became a nun and a missionary. In a crescendo of sacrificial love for Christ and his people, she chose voluntary martyrdom at concentration camp in Germany in 1945.

MARTYRIA AS FREEDOM

Martyrdom is said to be the truest witness of our beliefs. Death, as the last trial, eliminates the possibility of *masquerading* before God, oneself, people and the world. While there is room for "simulation" in one's practice of asceticism, the confrontation with death allows no room for such vanity. At the same time, the weak and the strong are equal in martyrdom: the ordinary Christian gains the same strength as the stronger one, and accepts suffering and death itself serenely and joyfully, receiving the crown of victory. The First Martyr, Christ, was not a passive victim but a *victor*, even in utter humiliation. Unjust verdict, slander, mockery, spitting, scourging, nailing to a cross, death and *weakness* were all transformed into *strength*. It can be said that the victory was achieved as much in the Resurrection as on the Cross (in the joyous apprehension of the great mystery), which is why we call Him Who bowed His head and fell asleep on the cross the *King of Glory*!

How is it then that Christians all too easily slip into hypocrisy? How can it be that those who have received grace and strength from God can fail so gravely and fall so foully? If a Christian can be referred to as a peculiar anthropological *type*, then we have an interesting phenomenon here. When he is virtuous, he far surpasses the most virtuous soul on earth (religious or non-religious), but when he sins, he far outranks the worst of non-Christian sinners. Jesus took a staunch stand against sanctimony. *Hypocrisy* allows us to hide our sinfulness from ourselves in a skillful way. Are not the sins that we deny in ourselves, refuse to recognize, greater than those of which we are conscious?

Present-day Christians—the ministerial priesthood of the hierarchy and the "royal priesthood" of the laity—should place less faith in their reasoning abilities and earnestly seek to think with the *mind of Christ*. In order to be able to accomplish this it is necessary, among other things, to look to the future—that is, to allow for the possibility that present judgments can be terribly *wrong*. Let us acknowledge that churches can be wrong. Over twenty years ago (January 15, 1998), the Patriarchate of Alexandria besought forgiveness from Saint Nectarios of Aegina because he was unjustly persecuted, accused and suspended from his bishopric in Cairo in 1889. Accusers of the saint failed to find any formal or theological reason for this punishment other than the observation that the young bishop did not fit within their specific *ambient* (climate). "If one would give me six lines written by the hand of the most honest man, I would find something in them to have him hanged," said Cardinal Richelieu. Yet, the afflictions that the Fathers speak of can help in many ways: when you lose your position you receive unforeseen blessings by being humble. Even through the arbitrary, *all-too-human* actions of Church representatives may appear scandalous and adverse in the eyes of the world, God, without condoning those actions, acts creatively, leading history towards its proper goal. God does not intervene in human affairs in the manner of *deus ex machina,* but "slowly and unfailingly" shows Himself as the righteous Judge.

Rejection of rational idols

I believe that the *apophatic* method in theology is one of the possible approaches that can lead to a more careful assessment of people and their actions. Apophaticism is an example of the relativization of both logocentric thinking and positivist moralism. Of course, it is not enough to be able to distinguish between apophatic and cataphatic theology. It is necessary to recognize the inner apophatic logic of existence. As Bishop Atanasije writes: "Our faith and being, almost all of our history and our present condition are apophatic, and apophaticism (not as a logical proclamation of truth about God, but as *participation* in this truth through prayer and liturgy) requires great intellectual and even greater spiritual effort and tenacity." As St. Barsanuphius said about the ancient Fathers: "Do not think that they, even if they were saints, could fully fathom the depths of God."

An example from neuroscience can help us understand that most of us, as a *rule,* are vulnerable to the illusory truth effect. We think our brain gives us a realistic picture of the world, but in fact it builds images based on conjectures. Just recently, an effective optical illusion went viral on the internet that succeeds in tricking the brain into seeing a color image. Upon a closer look, we see that the photo on the screen is actually black and white. (It does not appear black and white to most of us.) The effect is achieved by simply laying a grid of selectively colored lines over an original black-and-white image. What happens is that our brain—by inherent ways through inference, experience, association—colors the image in. Of course, it is known only *a posteriori* that in *reality* the image is not in color. The deeper lesson from this is that we, in almost every domain of life, make similar mistakes, and in so doing, still believe that we can fully grasp the reality of things. One of the comments on Twitter about this optical illusion said that this is how interpersonal relationships, negotiations, trade, politics and overall human communications work.

In painting, color is relational. The appearance of color is determined by the mutual influence of warm and cool hues; color does not exist in itself. In music, tone is about pitch, intensity, duration and "color." In all cases, it is about the interactive relation of the observer with the observed or the listener with the music. The recipient's personality (and brain) will fill in the gaps based on inherent assumptions, as mentioned above. Therefore, it is not always necessary to say everything in detail: if someone is a skilled speaker, he will make the desired impression without many words. The painter will reach a new artistic expression without many strokes (Byzantine iconography is a prime example of this kind of abstraction). Is this manipulation or relational reality? It is another way to express the reality of connections; that is, it is all about relational theology.

Does the Church value freedom or is freedom *Hybris*, that overbearing pride which leads to *Nemesis*? In Greek tragedy, ὕβρις is described as an overconfident goddess that provokes the anger of the gods and leads to νέμεσις, a well-deserved retribution. Historically, what were the implications if someone developed their own theological style, somewhat different from so-called *mainstream* theology, while at the same time not corrupting the Body of Christ with incorrect teaching? It seems that the situation was different than in our days. Specifically, we see that *the Church in the East did not judge or prohibit freedom of personal opinions*. It is said about St. Justin of Ćelije that, as a free and responsible member of the Church of Christ, he prophetically rebuked and criticized the official Church, writing critical letters to the Patriarch and the Synod of Bishops when needed. The church historian Bolotov observes: "Persons who are aflame with sincere love for the truth and the good of the Church, as was Gregory the Theologian, have sometimes run into serious doubts about the role of ecclesial bodies such as councils and synods."

Damnatio memoriae today

The Great Fathers of the Church sometimes criticized authoritarian church leadership, likening it to a disease. The critical words of Chrysostom or Gregory the Theologian on that account are too sharp for today's sensibility. Therefore, the words of historian Henry Adams, who described the effect of power as "a sort of tumor that ends by killing the victim's *sympathies*," sound neither new nor too metaphorical. Dacher Keltner, a professor of psychology at Berkeley, demonstrated by his research that individuals under the influence of power behave as if they have suffered a traumatic brain injury—becoming more impulsive, less aware of the risks of their decisions, and, crucially, they no longer see the world from other people's perspectives.

When the paramount motive behind theology is the salvation of God's creatures, then our words are not central. Bishop Atanasije (Jevtić), in his *Patrology*, says that in Christology, Cyril of Alexandria was guided primarily by soteriological reasons. "Amidst all the raging dispute, he is not obsessed with arguing over particular theological 'formulations,' he is not clinging to 'words' only. Moreover, he himself does not always pay strict attention to his words and expressions and does not always use them precisely and exactly in the same way." Dissidents from countries with totalitarian one-party political regimes have been persecuted for thinking differently, for using the "wrong" words, spoken, written or even gestured. Modern *damnatio memoriae* in some environments is gradual: a person is first silenced in institutions, followed by being banned from official forums. Reflecting on the collective trauma of persecution from Soviet Russia, the late Father Florovsky wrote in the 1930s: "It is especially tragic that several years ago, by the order of the Soviet authorities, a large group of Russian philosophers was expelled from their own country. They were exiled specifically as philosophers. This was a symbolic gesture, signifying the denial of creativity and freedom. Philosophy became useless and forbidden in Soviet Russia precisely because philosophical pathos and creativity are the expressions of spiritual freedom. The Soviet lifestyle, on the contrary, is a willful rejection and extinguishing of the free spirit."

Many young people today feel like one of the heroes from the Tennessee Williams drama *Cat on a Hot Tin Roof*, who movingly, tersely, confesses: "I'm not living with you. We occupy the same cage, that's all." Where there is no Christ, true relationships are lost, nothing makes sense any longer. This seems to be inadvertently depicted in Tarantino's latest movie *Once Upon a Time in Hollywood*. The irresistible impression while watching that movie's whole web of events (which occur at the height of counterculture and the hippie movement) is that there are no real human *relationships*.

The great Church Fathers and teachers never subjugated others, but left their followers free, telling them in the manner of St. Barsanuphius: "I have not bound you, brother, nor have I offered you a commandment, but only an opinion. Therefore, do as you please." Introducing the thought of the Church Fathers to his readers, Bishop Atanasije, like a true disciple of Fr. Georges Florovsky, wrote the following significant words: "Readers will see that among the recognized Church Fathers and writers there were some whose certain theological understandings were not in complete conformity with beliefs and experience of the Holy Church, but who were not condemned for that." When it comes to heretics, in the words of this leading Serbian theologian, "they were singled out as heretics not because they had their own personal opinions—the Church, at least in the East, neither condemned nor assaulted the freedom of personal opinion—but because they wounded and tore the unique Body of Christ, the Church, (like the seamless garment of Christ)."

Accent discrimination in theology

There have been many schools of thought in the history of the Church, and the Church has welcomed them. Schools, directions, trends ... all that was remains part of the unique Tradition. The real question of the relationship between various schools and their teachings in the ancient Church is reflected in the various answers provided regarding the *truth* about Christ's personhood. (For example, the Alexandrians rejected an autonomous humanity in Christ precisely because they could not conceive of man—in his true humanity realized in Christ—apart from communion with God). Occasionally, and unrelated to the two dominant schools of Alexandria and Antioch, a *new* and fresh theological approach would emerge, a "different angle" of observation, a new form to make the faith intelligible from theologians who considered themselves free to speculate where the Church had not delivered judgment. The Cappadocian school (if it may be so called) is representative here. The West also had its particular approach, as did the Syrian tradition.

But what we are interested in here is the fact that a different *accent* or emphasis in theology did not pose a problem. Throughout history, the practice of the Church has been to not interfere with the freedom of personal thought and speech but rather to eliminate apocrypha and forgeries. I believe that the time has come for a new generation to give birth to new expression. Expectations for this to happen have been laid out in the neo-patristic synthesis inaugurated by the ecumenical teacher Fr. Georges Florovsky. To accomplish this, it is necessary to find a way out of the current rigid and sterile scene, with the help of theologians who shape the theological *curriculum*, for they have learned that "the Kingdom of the heavens is like a man who is master of a house, who brings forth new and old from his treasury" (Matthew 13:52). We should not be saddened if, along the way, we sometimes fail in our efforts to become like our role models. Van Gogh tried *without success* to imitate Millet, whose work profoundly resonated with him (he was also inspired by Gauguin and Courbet). But it is comforting that, ultimately, Van Gogh found his own direction, and, in return, received something more valuable!

Modern theologians are called to engage in a "gigantomachy" concerning the critical issues of society and humanity. For example, the existential interpretation of dogma and theology that "speaks" the language of the modern world is a way of doing theology that is not rigidly *dogmatic* but rather offers a *creative resolution to life's problems*—fashioned after the neo-patristic approach to theology "for the life of the world." In this endeavor, theologians need not fear either science or philosophy, as the Fathers did not fear. They themselves incorporated certain Hellenistic, Neoplatonic elements, boldly and confidently using Plato, Stoicism, Philo, Origen where it suited, in order to express the "teaching of the Church." For example, there was no classic philosophical and literary work that young Constantine (Cyril, the Apostle to the Slavs) did not read and study at Photius' school. And that school was at the time described by Ignatius' supporters as a civilizational setback compared to Antiquity. This sounds paradoxical, does it not? However, as Fr. Matthew Baker has noted, Orthodox thought at the dawn of the twenty-first century shows as yet few indications of engagement with the culture of philosophical or scientific rationality—not to mention that of the arts and humanities.

In his book on the lives of the great symphonists called *Under a Sky Full of Violins (Der Himmel voller Geigen),* Rudolf Thiel says that many musicians conveyed with their lives the power of the musical revolution that flared up in their time, and which, in the beginning, was generally considered a "regress" or "recess." "New music of the symphonic era," he says, "has, nonetheless, emerged vigorously and quickly from this *opposition*, and the tide turned." On one occasion, when the snobs of his era ridiculed the Impressionists, Cézanne responded that, against all odds, he would ensure Impressionism a place in art museums.

The glory of the Church is the great symphony of the Resurrection and a direct testimony of that triumph. "When the apostles beheld the Resurrection of the Maker, they were amazed (ἐθαύμασαν), and sang the angelic praise. This is the glory of the Church; (αὕτη ἡ δόξα τῆς Ἐκκλησίας), this is the richness of the Kingdom," (Octoechos, tone 7, poem of John Damascus). As it was in the beginning with the first *martyrs* of the Resurrection and Pentecost (cf. Acts 2:32, "of which we are all *witnesses*"), so it is with the theologians of today who, filled with the pathos of freedom, continue to creatively testify to salvation in the Risen Lord by professing in our time the events of salvation from sacred history. No one will be able to discard a single stone that they have embedded into the Tradition.

August 11, in memory of the passing
of Fr. Georges Florovsky (1893–1979)

Metropolitan John Zizioulas,
acrylic on canvas, 2021, Bishop Maxim

An invisible axis connects the gaze of the depicted Metropolitan with the spectator. This gaze looks at us seriously and thoughtfully, and together with the soft wrinkles of the forehead and the ambiguous lips, seems to immobilize time, for it looks slightly away, as if penetrating our being and exploring something deep and hidden. The painter succeeded with great simplicity in expressing something ontological: the question of life and its meaning. The raised eyebrows of the portrait contribute to this. After all, this profound look seems to ask: do you really exist, spectator? Is this relationship real? In other words, they allow for hope to transpire in a relationship of the eyes that brings us into real relationship. It is what we say in theological language: a true eschatological loving relationship of persons.

THE WILL TO WILL

"Therefore I delight in frailties, in insults, in exigencies, in persecutions and ordeals for the sake of Christ." (2 Cor. 12:10)

Some believe that in artificial intelligence—when computer-controlled robots master the complex behavioral algorithms sufficiently—various human traits, such as awareness of beauty and humor, pain and pleasure, free will and conscience, will naturally manifest themselves. As we can read in Roger Penrose's *The Emperor's New Mind*, this is an incorrigibly naive notion. Free will can only be conceived in a non-deterministic world. But is this how things are in our world? Why is the concept of free will a stumbling block for the human mind?

There have been many great teachers of wisdom in the world. They have presented their sublime teachings on goodness, justice, love, truth, will, etc., in order to guide their followers in understanding how to lead ethical, virtuous lives. Yet none of those spiritual giants *personified* their teachings. No teacher has ever *personally* embodied the Truth he taught—except Christ. He *is* the hypostatic faith, truth, beauty, wisdom, love—and the hypostatic *will* of God. This adjective "hypostatic" is to be understood as Christ actualizing His will not as if merely moved by an impulse of His nature (natural reaction), but as the self-chosen and *self-willed* manifestation of His nature, determined by the personhood of the Son. In Christ, the will is not "instigated" by some neurological activity (though as a human being He possesses human physiology), but by way of "personal demonstration" (active participation). The ultimate demonstration occurred just before Golgotha. It was therefore possible for Him, when tortured, mocked and nailed upon a cross, to not react in a *natural* way (with rage, retaliation, etc.), but in His *personal* (hypostatic) manner of being; that is, by bestowing upon those who wronged Him the *freedom* which grants resurrection and eternal life. Let us conclude that Christ of His own volition transforms the impulses of nature into acts of will, so that they are not the result of natural necessity, as is the case with us. His hypostasis is not biological but—from our perspective—*eschatological*, since it is grounded on the interpersonal relationship among the three Persons of the Holy Trinity.

I would like to focus here on the notion of "demonstration," or verification. All that is precious is to be tried by fire. At the beginning of his ascetic endeavor, one monk prayed to God to give him the gift of love. His spiritual teacher (*staretz*) warned him to be careful what he prayed for, as it may be attended with *risk*. Before granting us anything, the Lord wants to *test* the heart. History is the arena in which this wrestling is played out, demonstrating the fickleness of human nature. Namely, if left only to natural processes, it is very unlikely that, as Florovsky wrote, the "will to will" along with a tremendous freedom in the awareness of one's creative duty and responsibility would awaken in the soul. In our world that pulsates with its own rhythms and presents itself as "completed" (but is not), the individual experiences his or her powerlessness. The brilliant sculptures of Alberto Giacometti (one of the most significant sculptors of the twentieth century) express that destiny (τὸ πεπρωμένο) through figures that remind one of lone barren trees in the winter. This is no wonder, for philosophical questions about the human situation, as well as existential and phenomenological debates, played a significant role in his work. In his book *The Philosophical Chasms*, Archimandrite Justin Popović, whose heart burned with the fire of divine love, said: "To exist in this mysterious world as a human being, is the first and biggest surprise." But the surprise can be unpleasant. The enchantment of cosmism lies at the core of this tragedy because man is surrounded and weighed down with mysteries. Man is small compared to the incomprehensible cosmos and his will proves weak. Yet, amidst such and similar views, the Fathers of the Church have developed an optimistic anthropology of will that considers man as a *macrocosm*. The seventh patristic century elevated the will to the place of highest prominence. How did that happen?

Already in the fourth century, one Church Father described man as a *macrocosm* in the microcosm, implying that man, being a godlike being, is potentially *larger* than the whole world. We can only imagine how much free will God has given him when he entrusted him with authority over creation, to manage it in accord with the principles He has established, tending inexorably towards God. Bearing in mind the importance of free will, Christian writers have come up with a wide range of expressions for the phenomenon of volition in human behavior (will, willingness, appetite, desire, yearning, determination, selection, choice, etc.). All of these concepts are different; θέλημα, for example, indicates power, and θέλησις indicates relationship.

To better understand the significance of the will, let us turn our attention to the fact that God, in the exercise of His will, "externalises" His *manner* of existence and operation. In the Holy Trinity there is no discriminating will, but the "divine and paternal (πατρικὸν) will" (according to one expression of St. Maximus the Confessor that sets the Father as the primary hypostasis of the common will), which is simple and shared by the Three Persons. At the same time, since created beings are the result of His free will, God knows all beings as His own will or his "desires." Unlike God, man, however, is a "willing being" in a conflicting (fallen) state. We all know how difficult it is for two strong-willed personalities to come to agreement; in this case *externalization* might be viewed as a threat to another being. Examples from married or monastic life can best illustrate this. There are subtle and obvious incongruities between the actual behavior of the world (including church authorities) and descriptions found in classic textbooks.

The unpredictable becomes the norm

In order to understand whether free will is an *illusion* created by our brains (convincing us that we made a free choice from the available options, whereas the choice has already been made for us), we must start from the fact that the very existence of the world is not really based on the nature or will of the world but on the will of the Other. God, however, "set forth the law" of man's capacity of free self-determination, according to one antinomic formulation of St. Gregory the Theologian. God thus establishes man's free will. Gregory wants to say that free choice is not only possible, but the necessary cause directing the flow of events. The nature of this will, however, needs to be explained.

For Maximus the Confessor, the natural will is a defining feature of human nature and is manifested in everyday *appetites* corresponding with the nature of the rational creature. The will is logical—that is, it is a self-chosen impulse and movement of reasoning. The will is also oriented toward that which is good, and seeks all that sustain nature. Thus, Maximus the Confessor defines it as an insatiable appetite. And while the will belongs to nature only as "a simple rational and vital desire," the will as a particular *mode* of willing, or a particular instance of purposive will oriented toward one thing or another, belongs to the human person, or *hypostasis*.

We also need to remember, however, that both St. Gregory of Nyssa and St. Maximus the Confessor believed that the will is the seat of sin. (The ancient Greeks did not associate sin with the will but with impurity.) The healing of human nature and the healing of the will are, therefore, two different things. The healing of nature happens through Christ's entire ministry that culminates in the resurrection. The purpose of healing the will, on the other hand, is in its inward transformation—which can only come from within, by *love*—an impossible feat for us to achieve without us.

Therefore, the concept of freedom cannot be reduced to merely the unhindered power of choice. Rather, freedom is a personal, *willed* and loving relationship with God, men and the world. The right will, therefore, is not one that oscillates between doing and not doing good. Moreover, the will's liberty is not about facing a *dilemma* of choice, but about the affirmation of our God-given logic. If freedom of choice is about goal-orientation—to be joined to that end for which our natures were originally formed—then we, as Christians, should not unthinkingly embrace an understanding of *freedom* as nothing but the unconstrained power of choice. Rather, it should be understood in the context of being *moved by love*.

The mystery of theology, as well as of art, lies in not knowing in advance what mode of reflection will be employed in the process. After all, to live a spiritual life is probably always connected with taking risks. In theology, the rule is that the *unpredictable* becomes the norm. There are, however, certain *constants* in theology that prevent the truth from being obscured. For example, truth cannot be found in falsehood, injustice, willfulness, bondage, punishment, or persecution. If possible, we should always avoid those who imagine they *own* the truth, that they have all the "facts" beforehand, and therefore are allowed to dominate the context... *Procul a Jove procul a fulmine* (far from Jupiter, far from his thunderbolt). Malevolence (or ill-will) is among the antipodes of the above concepts of the will; it is the road to anger, melancholy and a fall. The apostle Paul wrote to Titus (who was the bishop): "For it is necessary that a supervisor (bishop), as God's steward, be irreproachable—not *self-willed*, not vehement, not addicted to wine, not someone who resorts to blows, not prone to the sordid desire for financial gain" (Titus 1:7). God's grace transforms the will which, in the ascetic effort, saves a man from the "voluntarist" consequences of the Fall.

Theology as a lay service

Unlike wholly *self-willed* theologians, *charismatic* theologians do not claim to know how an illuminating thought arises. As Picasso observed, every painter, even graduate painter, is an "amateur" when he starts a painting. We can say the same for every theologian—that he is an "amateur" (lay) theologian when he starts an academic systematization of his thought. When John Zizioulas reflects on a theological theme, he resembles a child who speaks freely and fervently to listeners about what he has seen and experienced. When a child draws a picture, they do it without fear of making mistakes; they draw lines as if they know exactly what the picture will look like. It is the same when they sing. It is a gift.

A child's *imagination* reminds us that φαντασία (imagination), in the anthropological sense, is an essential characteristic of the will, which is affirmed as the possibility to exceed ourselves by re-directing our will toward the *blessed* goal. After all, each of the beatitudes are given from the perspective of the future (cf. Matthew 5:3-11). Imagination represents an opportunity a person is given in order to set *goals* while surpassing his *powers* and his *authority* (by which he is in contradiction with himself), and in that way to *innovate* his will. The Fathers teach us that we truly have integrity only if we have the love that leads the will to no longer oppose our God-given nature.

When we enter the realm of truth, the darkness disappears because "At the coming of grace, the shadow of the law passed away" (παρῆλθεν ἡ σκιὰ τοῦ νόμου, τῆς χάριτος ἐλθούσης). The truth also illuminates the darkness. The Greek painter Yannis Tsarouchis once said that "on the Attica peninsula, at noon, bodies soak up the shadows." It requires a special sensitivity to be able to make such a keen observation. When we surrender to the "Spirit that has neither beginning nor end," we become free and notice that one virtue attracts and prepares the heart for another. Similarly, when a person commits a sin, another sin follows (for example, *lying* about committing the first sin in order to avoid the consequences).

Christ, as the eternal Logos of God the Father in the Holy Spirit, is the Person in whom God's uncreated *logoi*-wills of creation "reside". He acts in history in such a way that all generations can willingly accept the mystery of his personal incarnation as an eschatological designation, so that their "Yes" may be an eternal "Yes" (cf. James 5:12).

***Father Dumitru**: The Theologian of the Prisons*,
acrylic on canvas, 2021, Bishop Maxim

Fr. Dumitru Staniloae "sits in silence, with no wish to speak" (Saint Silouan), recalling the joy of life in prison as described by Elder Sofian Boghiu: "I can say that I had days, many days, in prison that were more joyful than outside, because joy comes from within, not from outside." He remembers entering his cell and seeing other inmates writing biblical verses from memory on their boot soles–verses which he as a professor of theology had not yet inscribed on the tablet of his heart; he longs for the unceasing prayer God granted him amidst the inhumane tortures and deprivations; he gazes upon God's suffering people, wishing to console them through the living, grace-filled theology welling up in his heart, through the experience of Christ Whom he met within the four walls of a prison cell.

NOMADIC HUMILITY AND COURAGE

Trypho, a religious Jew, is reported to have said to St. Justin the Philosopher and Martyr: "I am aware that your precepts in the so-called Gospel are so wonderful and so great, that I suspect no one can keep them" (*Dialogue with Trypho*, Ch. 10). (St. Justin was one of the earliest Christian apologists and lay theologians, and this interfaith dialogue occurred in the second century.) How valid was Trypho's point of view? Even a cursory glance at the history of Christianity certainly seems to justify his opinion. After all, we do not have to look long and hard to see that Christians sin at every turn. Even a superficial look at the Sermon on the Mount—which teaches that a man has already sinned in his heart by looking at a woman and lusting for her (Matthew 5:22-28), and invites disciples to sell everything they have and give to the poor—shows that we cannot reduce the precepts of Christ to a mere ethical system. Why? Because the teachings do not call for a general improvement in behavior, but the "dying" of the ego through the negation of the ego, and emphasize the absolute primacy of the Other (God and neighbor) over the selfish *I*.

I have always wondered why some "great" spiritual teachers cannot find a way to overcome egoism and so refrain from reciprocating in kind when they feel that someone has stepped on their toes. How come they do not rather choose to forgive and say something like, "let us rise above human weaknesses," because love surpasses all? Today's "institutional" prelates do not follow the logic of the Sermon on the Mount. No one is even surprised when those greats of the "virtuous" life respond harshly, even antagonistically, to even the most well-meaning criticism. It shows that instead of overcoming one's ego, ascetic effort may even lead to its affirmation. Someone has made an observation that a person can be a thief and still retain a sense of humanity, whereas someone considered to be a "spiritual" person may become devoid of humanity. When the courage to confront the truth face-to-face disappears from spiritual institutions, it leads to a downplaying and denial of the problem, or to its misrepresentation (e.g. making it seem less ugly).

In contrast to this negative phenomenon of the "spiritual priesthood," one great second century Bishop—when in his hundredth year and on the route to Rome where he met his martyrdom—uttered these poignant words: "Now I begin to be a disciple" (νῦν ἄρχομαι μαθητὴς εἶναι). St. Ignatius of Antioch was sent to the arena in the capital of the *Imperium Romanum* to be devoured by the beasts, but in all the places through which he passed, he encouraged Christians with words of advice. In the last year of his life, this extraordinary man became a kind of Christian "nomad martyr."

Nomads as servants of theology

Is it a curse or a privilege to live in a nomadic state? As some research shows, the future of science or progress lies "beyond one's county's borders." Science is often better served by researchers who live outside their home countries (it is not by accident that a large number of Nobel laureates have lived and died outside their homelands). Does this apply to theologians?

If we disregard the reasons for their migration to different countries and take a closer look at their personal names, it becomes both obvious and surprising how many theological giants of the academic world fall into the category of expatriate, nomad theologians. Originally from Odessa, G. Florovsky reached New York and Boston via Prague, Belgrade and Paris. Alexander Schmemann and John Meyendorff followed their own routes westward. Elder Sophrony Sakharov went from Russia to Europe, then to Mount Athos, only to establish a monastery in England that today shines with spirituality on everyone. And what about Bishop Anthony Bloom or Metropolitan John Zizioulas? Both have gained reputations as foremost theologians in the U.K. Nicholai Velimirović became more renowned in America than in Serbia: in 1946, he was awarded the honorary degree of Sacred Theology from Columbia University, yet never received an honorary doctorate from the University of Belgrade.

What can intuitively be taken as an important factor here is "mobility." As one pursues his dream, traveling across geographical and national borders, an interesting process of self-introspection begins, once the fear of risk-taking has been overcome by courage. It has been noted that the concept of mobility has become so important in some areas of life that moving up the academic ladder is almost impossible without relocating to a foreign country. In her essay entitled *Crossing Oceans* (2012), Eve Marder equated scholars who take risks and go abroad with those early explorers whose travels "shaped their views of the world, and the tales they told expanded the universe for all those they encountered." Of course, this does not mean that I endorse the elitism of the privileged, who travel abroad only if guarantees can be furnished. But the fact remains that an insecure spirit feels even more insecure in unfamiliar circles, on unfamiliar playgrounds. Emigrants know this best. Christianity can be viewed, with some exceptions, as a cultural and civilizational phenomenon; it does not only contribute to the culture of a city, it *is*, after all, the culture of a city.

The benefits of crossing a border or an ocean are undoubtedly great. If you have managed to overcome an inferiority complex, graduate and postdoctoral studies abroad offer opportunities to prove your independence, discover a different culture, and follow those best in the profession, wherever they may be. Moreover, networking creates connections that often prove invaluable in later years. Over the past twenty years, personal and professional affiliations have played a large role in creating opportunities for the Orthodox audience to hear the most brilliant theological minds of today. Nomad theologians—or those who go abroad for research purposes—have shown through their sacrifice where dedication can lead and how far willpower can take us. Of course there are, indeed, many things to beware of—there are dangerous places and drawbacks along every spiritual path. However, the most important struggle remains the one against one's ego.

A freedom that laughs at death

The ascetic treatise known as *The Ladder of Divine Ascent*, written by John Climacus in ca. 600 AD, provides an excellent example of how the question of the role of the ego has been tackled in the ascetic tradition. It describes the way in which the spirituality of the Church cultivates an ethos of grace and humility; that is, how conquering one's ego helps in overcoming ideas of "superiority." "Forget your good deeds as soon as possible," was the advice that St. Nicholai of Zhicha gave to his contemporaries. In *The Ladder*, for instance, we read about a monk who, having suffered an insult, remained completely still in his heart and prayed internally; yet he then began to weep over being offended, hiding his dispassion (*apatheia*) with pretended passion. In contrast to the tendency of the modern man to pretend not to long for prominence while being obsessed with a burning desire to dominate, Climacus speaks of "another of the brethren who had no longings at all for the office of superior pretended that he was working for this." Here we encounter the ethos of a man who is ready to give his place to another, not deny it to him. "And how am I to describe the chastity of that man who went into a brothel ostensibly for the sake of sin, but drew the harlot to the ascetic life?" These ascetics fought even against demons, offering themselves as manifestations of the transforming Christ-like freedom that laughs at death. "Again, a bunch of grapes was brought very early in the morning to one of the hermits, and after the person who brought them had gone, he ate them with a semblance of gobbling but without any pleasure, to make it seem to the demons that he was a glutton." Those are the kind of people who are not overly concerned with their own reputation and social standing, but strive to deceive the enemy by overcoming the ego, like a monk who, "having lost a few palm-leaves he used for making baskets, spent all day pretending that he was grieved about this." Such ascetics, by maintaining ontological humility—because psychological humility alone is not enough—can outsmart demons whose only objective is to confuse and divert many from the truth. St. John Climacus makes a final comment with them in mind: "It was of these, no doubt, that the Apostle said: As both deceivers and truthful men." (2 Corinthians 6:8)

All of these cases of "deceivers" tell us that by accepting a certain way of life (a specific ethos), one does not becomes "entitled" or "deserving" of anything over and above others. Instead of instructing us how to correct ourselves and others with love, the "institutional" clergy have obliterated the ethos of the ancient *Ladder* casually and recklessly as if erasing the letters on the chalkboard. And let us not think lightly that many voices of freedom, which brave a bold rebellion against counterfeits and delusions in the Church itself, have been extinguished. What is to be done about such a sad state of affairs? I believe that the solution is to endeavor to preserve that which is worthwhile. (Tarantino managed to do this in his new movie *Once Upon a Time in Hollywood*, as did South Korean Bong Jun-Ho in *Parasite*).

One account from the life of Saint Gregory Palamas offers us timely advice. In his third year at the hermitage of Saint Sabbas on Mount Athos, in a state of prayer, Gregory Palamas fell into a light sleep and experienced a vision in which he was encouraged to share the wisdom bestowed upon him from on high. It seemed to him that in his hands was a vessel overflowing with milk. Then this milk took the form of wine, which flowed over the brim of the vessel onto his hands and clothes, spreading abroad a wonderful fragrance. As soon as Gregory perceived it, he was filled with holy joy. There appeared to him a radiant youth who said, "Why do you not pass on this wonderful drink, left by you without due attention. This is the ever-inexhaustible gift from God." "To whom should I pass on this drink when there is no one in need of it?" asked Saint

Gregory. "Even if at the present moment there is no one actually thirsting for the drink," answered the youth, "yet, nevertheless, you should do your duty and not neglect this gift of God. With the proper use of which, you will have to answer before God" (cf. Matt. 25:14-30). With these words the wondrous vision came to an end.

This example shows that the blessing of theology conceals great dynamism in every moment, even when things seem hopeless. It is only when one is drawn to the path of voluntary mortification, as if being buried in the "good earth," that the new person can emerge. It cannot emerge if one is a timid, facile person, nor will one unleash the forces of dynamism of one's being by "normalizing" problems. When we die for Christ, we truly live.

Responsible exercise and experience of inner freedom is characterized by being able to call things by their proper names, not by suffocating precious sincerity behind the closed doors of our rooms. Life cannot be fully experienced until we stop venerating false authorities. The cross we take up is the "invincible weapon and the solid ground of the faith."

The church is not a mere hospital, but also a place where we "die in order to live," so that we can become bold toward the Lord and others, not to our judgment or condemnation. When we understand this, the seed of our being will sprout and bear fruit and produce a crop—a hundredfold. Only then will the doubting Tryphos of the 21st century believe that it is possible for the true people of Christ to keep His commandments.

Kallistos Ware,
acrylic on canvas, 2022, Bishop Maxim

A peaceful look, without the need to control. As if experiencing the weight of the blessing given to him, the Bishop lifts the blessed weight of the Divine gift he has received and says: "For my yoke is easy, and my burden is light." Kallistos Ware is an English bishop and theologian, under the Ecumenical Patriarchate of Constantinople. From 1966 to 2001, he was Spalding Lecturer of Eastern Orthodox Studies at the University of Oxford.

***An African Child*,**
acrylic on canvas, 2021, Bishop Maxim

Traditional characteristics of African children, such as early maturity in self-discipline, early search for identity, and a spirit of cooperation and interdependence, are discernable in this portrait. Peter Paul Rubens explored a variety of facial expressions and poses of a black person. Using a single dim source of light, he created strong contrasts of brightness and shadow on the man's skin, varying these along with the different expressions.

CHRIST AS SOJOURNER AND STRANGER

Every year as we journey toward Christmas and the small cave in Bethlehem, the attention of modern Christians is habitually directed toward folklore, ritual and recipes, gushy songs, perfectly wrapped gifts, and the like. The current migrant crisis, however, prompts us to remember the *migrant* dimension of Christmas. Our God before the ages, without leaving the Fathers' bosom, was forced, while still in the womb of the holy Virgin, to seek *shelter* with Mary and Joseph, first in the vicinity of Bethlehem and then in Egypt. Remembering those poignant scenes from the life of the greatest Migrant, and through Him realizing our real status in the world, pushes us to understand more deeply the problem of migrants and refugees in our day.

In addition to a dramatic human identity crisis and problems concerning our relationship with the environment, the migrant crisis is perhaps the most serious problem of humanity today. This problem reconnects the West with the East in a dramatic way, urging deep reflection on the issue of human responsibility in the world. Thus, Christians join forces to solve this problem, too.

It is sad that, in most cases, (im)migrants are viewed as "excess people"; since there is *no place* for them, they are therefore rendered superfluous. Dismayed by the news of refugees being treated as "excess," an iconographer, Stamatis Skliris started to paint "The Surplus People" on a dark canvas. In doing so, he joined the small number of Orthodox painters who experience the emergence of migrants as a call to repentance for neglecting their distressing fates. In Stamatis' painting we see Christ among the migrants floating in the water beside an overcrowded boat, somewhere in the Mediterranean. Christ is a fellow-refugee Who participates in the plight of all, without exception, through his own exile and martyrdom on the Cross. Those who have already drowned are painted with bright and clam faces as if telling us that they have overcome fear and death. In the years to come, the composition "The Surplus People" will likely receive even darker tones. Will Orthodox Christians manage to add lighter shades to it?

The state of hospitality today

At the Naples Conference dedicated to interreligious dialogue and migration in the context of the Mediterranean area held in June 2019, the Ecumenical Patriarch Bartholomew stated in an alarming tone that "the Lord's commandment to welcome strangers is in danger," alluding to certain governments and countries that have disallowed desperate migrants from finding any kind of refuge. The problem of immigration, like other problems today, should bring Christians closer.

There are some ambiguities about the term "refugee" or migrant. This mass phenomenon has become a systemic feature of the globalized world. A migrant, as I have said, is regarded as "human surplus," which—by the very nature of *excess*—manifests the arrogance of those who are not among the folk counted as "surplus." The theological dimension of the *neighbor*, however, can certainly help provide perspective in the context of the contemporary humanitarian crisis and the character of globalization. *Acceptance* of the weakest, exposed to social and economic pressures, is imperative. This undoubtedly requires theological criteria: without a theological sensibility, the response to the crisis may be wrong. In this historic hour, in light of the way the refugee crisis is unfolding, people of influence should act in the spirit of the Gospel.

It has been pointed out already in the *Epistle to Diognetus* that, paradoxically at first sight, Christians should perceive every country (and no country) as their "fatherland." Likewise, the apostle Paul spoke in the letter to the Philippians (3:20) about the eschatological citizenship that is yet to come. In the *Republic*, Plato brought up the idea that the cities in which we dwell are an image—and a distorted one, a poor copy—of the inner man (IX, 592b). The challenge of living in diaspora reminds the Orthodox of the Church's passenger status in the world, *in via*, since "we are in the world but not of the world." This is why Orthodoxy resists idolatrous attitudes toward the concepts of "homeland," "fatherland" and nation.

The Biblical view of strangers

Many have opined that the entire Biblical story is actually a *migration* story. Both the Old and New Testaments tell poignant histories of exiles who were forced to flee their homes. Although the term "refuge" cannot be found in the Bible, there are many sections that speak of "strangers," "aliens," or "foreigners." The most famous migration story is found in the book of Exodus, which tells the story of the children of Israel who were victims of ruthless slavery in Egypt. Although nearly hopeless, they were able to escape and find refuge in the desert led by God's mighty hand. For forty years they lived wandering the desert without a permanent abode. But, in the end, God fulfilled the promise that He made and settled them on a land they could finally call home.

Because their experience of homelessness, displacement and alienation was so painful, God commanded His people to always show special care to foreigners: "When a stranger sojourns with you in your land, you shall not do him wrong. You shall treat the stranger who sojourns with you as the native among you, and you shall love him as yourself, for you were strangers in the land of Egypt" (Leviticus 19:33–34). Hospitality is a concrete example of love for these "strangers" as well as an indication of how God's people should live: it always make room for the stranger.

At the very beginning of the New Testament, in the Gospel of Matthew, we find the story of Joseph and

Mary fleeing into Egypt with their newborn son, Jesus, because of the envy of the paranoid Emperor Herod. Our Savior spent his early childhood as a refugee because his country was not safe for Him. Furthermore, in the Gospel of Luke, Christ is described as a "stranger" and "foreigner" in this world (2:4, 39; 4:29–30; 8:1; 9:53, 58;13:22; 17,11; 24:18), which emphasizes his hypostatic connection to the whole world even more. "The foxes have lairs and birds of the sky have nests, but the Son of Man has no place where he may rest his head" (Matthew 8:20).

Drawing on the experience of Israel, Christ stresses the Old Testament commandment of love for the alien in their midst (Isaiah 58:7) as a criterion against which everyone will be judged: "For I was hungry and you gave me something to eat, I was thirsty and you gave me drink, I was a stranger, and you gave me hospitality" (Matthew 25:35).

Baptism as the acceptance of migrant status

The Bible challenges us by calling us to love those who are *different* from us, and not to hide in the safety zone of our privacy, surrounding ourselves with people who never challenge our views. "For if you love only those who love you, what recompense do you have? ... And if you greet only your brothers, what are you doing that is extraordinary? Do not even the Gentiles do so?" (Matthew 5:46–47).

One of the necessary consequences of baptism is the knowledge of the truth that the "new man" has no "father" on earth, for there is one who is our heavenly Father (Matthew 23:9) and our "brothers and sisters" are members of the Church. Similarly, this "new man" has no citizenship on earth but in the heavens (Philippians 3:30) since his "city" is the one "about to come" (Hebrews 13:14; ἀλλὰ τὴν μέλλουσαν ἐπιζητοῦμεν), the future Kingdom. In this way, the Christian *is* and *is not* a stranger at the same time. This is the existential meaning of Baptism as the "death" of the "old man" and the birth of the "new"; the Christian has an eschatological personality. According to this teaching, no one is an immigrant and all of us are immigrants, in one or another sense.

Christ is the great Stranger in history, the gracious Samaritan who shakes the foundations of existing monolithic societies by accepting sinners into the community, in anticipation of his eschatological meal. In doing so, Jesus introduces a different ethos and logic with which he "defines" his people, his friends, his family, his mother, and his brothers. What defines them henceforth is not the blood relation, nor common goals (national, political or economic), but a love that creates and sustains and renews. "Whoever does the will of God, this one is my brother and sister and mother" (Mark 3:35).

The Gospel suggests that unless we recognize Christ in the person of the stranger or foreigner, or the sick, the poor, the prisoner, then, in fact, we do not know him at all. The stranger is the hidden Christ among the community. For example, St. Gregory the Theologian encouraged his listeners not to flee from lepers (i.e., outcasts from society): "You will not demean yourself in the process ... extend a helping hand, offer food, give old clothes, provide medicine, bandage wounds, ask after them, counsel fortitude, offer encouragement, keep them company" (*Oration* 14, 27). Just as God sends "rain upon the just and the unjust" (Matthew 5:45), so the saints of the Church see everyone as pure and innocent. To them, there are no strangers and newcomers. Moreover, they are closest to those who are lost and tormented because the saints see themselves as unworthy and lost.

Historical circumstances and risks

One can argue that the center of gravity of a particular culture is revealed in the way it deals with the problem of foreigners (newcomers, immigrants and strangers). Images of the crucified Christ are all around us today: on ships carrying migrants and refugees, among victims of human trafficking, among immigrants being beaten on the streets of European capitals, among prisoners in concentration camps. Thus, today's "biblical" strangers are asylum seekers, displaced persons, refugees, migrants (those who permanently leave their home countries because of poverty), immigrants (those who go to another country seeking a better life), exiles, stateless persons ... It is for this reason that Patriarch Bartholomew has urged that the separation of economic migrants from asylum seekers in Europe be stopped.

Serious questions nevertheless arise over the nature of the global turmoils of our time. Some of them closely resemble those more brutal historical events. Over the course of years in the development of European civilization, from the end of the fourth to the seventh century, much of Western Europe experienced a cultural *upheaval* that disrupted the Greco-Roman heritage. New tribes, on their way to Europe where they eventually settled—the Goths, Huns, Franks, Vandals, Normans, Slavs—lived at a very low cultural level. This period was euphemistically called the "Great Migration of Nations," but it was a violent and mass migration with enormous historical consequences: for instance, the reality of the *city* was destroyed. In this sense, the Christian obligation to accept strangers should not eliminate the moral obligation to address the roots and causes of mass migration of people today. Although everyone has the right to seek a safe and humane life, no country is obliged to accept *all* those who wish to live in it. The migrant crisis does not cease to be one of the most politically polarizing topics in both Western Europe and America.

Response from the Diaspora

In his *New Sermons at the Foot of the Mount*, St. Nicholai of Zhicha raises a curious question: "Why did Christianity first spread almost exclusively in a westward direction? Why did not the resurrected Lord send his apostles to the east rather than the west, where the road was narrow and dangerous?" Nicholai finds the answer in the challenge of living in unfamiliar places: "Christ was a stranger in the West. Through His disciples, He undertook a journey on the narrow and dangerous road."[1]

It seems to me that contemporary theology has not given proper importance to the *immigrant* status of the Church. This is also apparent in widespread misunderstandings of many areas of Christian life. For example, many believers attach importance to their national heritage; in theology, the emphasis is given to the original state of man; in academic theology, to historical paradigms; and in worship, the "movement towards the end" has almost ceased. It is as if sometimes Christians themselves are slowing down their journey to the Kingdom of God.

It is no coincidence, however, that the so-called Orthodox diaspora has rediscovered this forgotten dimension. During the 1970s and 1980s, Orthodox theologians in America began to delve into the Church's

[1] Conversely, in his book *The Lost History of Christianity* Philip Jenkins argues that a thousand years ago Asia and Africa were more Christian than Europe.

post-immigrant identity and helped lay the foundations for social ethics and missiology in this democratic, religiously pluralistic, and increasingly secular society. New trends in Orthodox theology are the result of activities in the diaspora, especially by Russian immigrants in Europe after the Soviet Revolution.

Although the diaspora (as an unavoidable challenge to the old and new Israel) is one of the most complex problems in the entire Orthodox world, it is also a great blessing: it reminds us of the truth concerning the Church's itinerant, temporary status in the world, and that she should live under the cross daily. The voyage to the Kingdom should determine what choices we make on Earth. The "Orthodox diaspora" is the only reliable link with today's *oikoumenē*.

An important task of Orthodox theology today is to put the "theology of neighbor" in the common, interactive milieu of ideas and reflection. Our theology is not protological but eschatological. Nostalgia for the Land of the Living is nostalgia inspired by the future. Eschatological nostalgia is not a romantic craving for the past, as in Hellenistic and Hindu religions which, as Eliade put it, were "prisoners of their own archetypal intuitions."

It is therefore not surprising that Orthodox parishes in the diaspora were regarded as true asylums and shelters for newcomers. In the entire history of the Church in the Diaspora, from the first immigrants to the latest waves of immigration, parishes (*paroikia*) were the heart and soul of the immigrant communities, so much so that the founding of the parish was the biggest step in the religious and social life of immigrants.

The sharing of the Eucharistic Bread reveals the energetic renewal of social compassion that results from liturgical transformation. When the Apostle Paul wrote to the Hebrews, reminding them in chapter 13 to not neglect hospitality to strangers, "for thereby some have entertained angels unaware" (he was referring primarily to Abraham receiving three Angels in his house), he showed that the true and only foundation of Christian charity is the same one that leads to understanding God: one must first be a *person*.

Fyodor Dostoevsky,
acrylic on canvas, 2021, Bishop Maxim

“Dostoevsky’s face is the face of a peasant. An ashen hue pervades the hollow cheeks, making them appear almost grimy, emphasizing the furrows caused by many years of suffering ... To right and left, two huge boulders jut forth, the prominent cheekbones typical of his race; a sparse moustache and a straggling beard veil the sad-looking mouth and delicate chin. All is dark and preeminently earthly in this unbeautiful face. I have called it a peasant’s, but I might almost term it a beggar’s, so flat and colorless is it, so lacking in brightness: a piece of the Russian steppe cast high and dry upon the stones”. (*Dostoevsky* by Stefan Zweig)

DOSTOEVSKY AS MESSENGER OF LIFE

In 2021, the world celebrated the bicentenary of the birth of Fyodor Mikhailovich Dostoevsky (born November 11, 1821, Moscow, died February 9, 1881, Saint Petersburg). This is an important anniversary of a Russian novelist and short-story writer whose psychological penetration into the darkest recesses of the human heart, coupled with his unparalleled moments of illumination, left no one indifferent—neither his contemporaries nor later generations. We will thus celebrate the anniversary of a writer who calls things by their proper names without presuming to judge, and who never ceases to perplex us, leaving us to untangle conundrums through our own wits. By sayings such as "one feels suffocated without a goal in life," or "happiness does not come from earthly comforts, but is earned through suffering," or "beauty will save the world," or "truth without love is a lie," Dostoevsky has made an indelible spiritual imprint on all generations. He left behind important reminders that our ideals will always collide with our limitations and that we need help from above, given the fact that we are profoundly fragile creatures.

How should one celebrate Dostoevsky's anniversary? By throwing a gala event? By publishing scientific papers? Or, when it comes to this great Russian and European writer in whose person the East and the West met, would it perhaps not be more appropriate to let his heroes speak from the pages of his books, from theatres in Petersburg, Zurich, Nanjing, and New York? I would like this text to be a modest but timely introduction to a 200th jubilee, an attempt to pave the way for a new reading of the works of this great Russian writer.

André Gide wrote that "though pregnant with thought, Dostoevsky's novels are never abstract, indeed, of all the books I know, they are the most palpitating with life." Dostoevsky's pen, sharp but compassionate, melancholy and lovely, is something sorely needed in our age that gullibly clings to the idea that science can save us (one that disgusted him), and that technology can make us perfect. In *Homo Deus* (2016), Noah Yuval Harari warned what could happen if a person combined algorithms with artificial intelligence and genetic engineering. Already in 1864, the hero of *Notes from the Underground* warned that if human actions could be tabulated according to laws of natures—mathematically, like tables of logarithms—then life would be reduced to solving quadratic equations, and everything would be so clearly calculated and explained that there would be no more incidents or adventures in the world. In *The House of the Dead* we find these consoling words, "neither the branding irons nor chains will make him forget that he is a man."

Dostoevsky leads us to a more humane truth perceived by the great sages: freedom is the most precious gift, and life is, and always will be, marked with suffering. In his prodigious literary works, Fyodor refers to repentance and redemption as preconditions of becoming God-like.

The fruit of the Gospel seed

In Dostoevsky's literary works the seeds of the theology of the Church Fathers were sown, which Byzantium had originally sown in the Russian soil from the earliest time of its conversion to Christianity. It has long been observed that over the centuries these seeds have yielded such great fruit that they have nourished not only the soul of the Russian people but the soul of modern people throughout the world. Having sprung out of the bosom of the Russian Church, Dostoevsky, with his anti-sentimental spirit, transformed that seed into nourishment for all people.

Exactly what kind of seeds are those? Here are just some of the questions that Dostoevsky addressed: the human heart as the seat of freedom, love for the earth, suffering, repentance, the authoritarian (inquisitorial) syndrome of the subordination of human conscience, beauty, atheism, Europe, boredom as "hell," the desolation and meaninglessness of life, Christ as one of us, a "living life," pilgrimage, man in the light of encounter with the Lord, objective truth, love before logic, "small people," isolation, the Slavic soul, humanity, saints and sinners, the Optina elders, theodicy, incarnation, the tragedy of evil, doubts, passions, temptations, judgment, obedience (meekness), and many others. It is also apparent that Dostoevsky made a personal commentary on the Holy Fathers. Those better acquainted with the tradition of the Philokalia point out that its Slavonic translation resulted in the emergence of a very dynamic movement among Russian intellectual circles. This is precisely what later gave rise to a large-scale movement called the "philokalian renaissance," conceived in the provincial monastery of Optina. This movement first exerted influence on the group of "Slavophile" intellectuals, and later on the great Russian writers and intellectuals, such as Tolstoy, Solovyov and especially Dostoevsky (it suffices to look at the chapter "Elders" in *The Brothers Karamazov*).

This great novelist has had a profound influence on literary modernism, existentialism, many philosophers (Nietzsche acknowledged that Dostoevsky was the only one from whom he had something to learn), various schools of psychology, as well as theology and literary criticism. Everyone wants to claim him. For Dostoevsky, reason and harmony are not the supreme goals of human life. The hero from the underground clearly points this out: "And how do these wiseacres know that man wants a normal, a virtuous choice? What has made them conceive that man must want a rationally advantageous choice? What man wants is simply independent choice, whatever that independence may cost and wherever it may lead..." (*Notes from the Underground*).

Freedom as rebellion

Freedom, in contrast to dry rationalism, allowed Dostoevsky (who, by observing people in a prison setting, revised his earlier, "progressive" views) to tackle several Christian themes. In the first place, he specifically addressed man's relationship to suffering: "Man is sometimes extraordinarily, passionately, in love with suffering ..." According to him, "Pain and suffering are always inevitable for a large intelligence and a deep heart. The really great men must, I think, have great sadness on earth." This is by no means an apotheosis of misery or a justification of sadomasochism (although the author does occasionally speak of "love" that hurts others). For example, *The House of the Dead* is not an apology of suffering. Rather, the author merely pleads that it is better to be a victim than a hangman: "In the world where everything is distorted, soiled, there is nothing left for the victim but to turn suffering into a virtue, gain a moral advantage over the tyrant," observed Milosav Babović (literary historian and translator from the Russian text). Dostoevsky's heroes, however, are not appeased and do not come to terms with their lot in life or with their torturers (cf. the novel *Humiliated and Insulted*). The focus is more on the gateway to finding freedom in suffering. (Dostoevsky raises the question in almost all his works: suffering serves as a proof of man's independence, of him being alive and having the power to renounce even his own happiness in the name of freedom.) Metropolitan John Zizioulas observed that such an approach unlocks the secret of human freedom as the ability to acknowledge one's inability to fully know and understand the other. Such personalities as we meet in Dostoevsky's works can turn their weakness into strength and exercise their power in powerlessness. Yet, if understood outside of Christology, any advocacy of this subject leads to nihilism. Dostoevsky, on the other hand, is the herald of the gospel message. Just as Christ died and was resurrected, so does man gain true life through dying.

This is where the biblical story about the grain of wheat comes more fully into view. Unless the grain of wheat falling to the ground dies, it remains alone; but if it dies it bears plenteous fruit (John 12:24). Dostoevsky used these words of Christ as an epigraph to his greatest work, *The Brothers Karamazov.* Bishop Atanasije (Jevtić) finds the key to interpreting Dostoevsky in the willingness of his heroes to die. "The test of faith is readiness to die, as new life will come from death; if his heroes are receptive to that truth—regardless of whether they have achieved something or failed at something, or even (or especially) if they have failed to live up to that truth—the seed of eternal life has already been planted in their hearts." Precisely because he had a very difficult life (convicted for his political views, placed before a firing squad, sentenced to four brutal years in a Siberian prison, and then required to endure another two years in the army), Dostoevsky was able to masterfully present this Parable of the Grain of Wheat—one that he understood better than anyone else—as an indispensable subject of reflection about life's most important questions.

At the heart of Dostoevsky's thought is what we might clumsily call his existential Christology, which the Russians have traditionally nurtured. Voluntary self-emptying (*kenosis*) leads to the cross; the experience of salvation takes place in the heart of the sinner. And just as Dostoevsky believed that one is purified by suffering, so did Saint Silouan of Athos in our time when in his soul he heard: "Keep your mind in hell and do not despair."

Longing for life

The next big topic is Dostoevsky's passion for life, which is transformed into the most abundant life (Gide). The dialogue between Alyosha and Ivan Karamazov reveals the spiritual lucidity of the great writer: "I am awfully glad that you have such a longing for life," cried Alyosha. "I think everyone should love life above everything in the world." "Love life more than the meaning of it?" "Certainly, love it, regardless of logic as you say, it must be regardless of logic, and it's only then one will understand the meaning of it." (*The Brothers Karamazov* V, III). Because he had felt a passionate attachment to life during his imprisonment,

Dostoevsky became an eloquent advocate of the joy of life for the remainder of his days.

As the direct opposite to natural religiosity, Dostoevsky portrays the faith of the Church as the boldness of freedom in contrast to "faintness of heart." The three pillars of power—miracle, mystery and authority—in his view deprive man of freedom. These are the three established practices of institutionalized religion, and Dostoevsky referred to them as factors of (in Yannaras' words) "voluntary renunciation of one's own freedom, its betrayal by being enslaved by passions, by unconditional submission." In presenting his conception of a man of "faint heart" or religious pietism, Dostoevsky correctly states: "Open his prison and give him freedom, and he will tie himself up and come crawling back." Do we not see this today in both secular and church circles? Therefore, the overall oeuvre of our writer is summed up as an effort to restore the Christ of the Church in place of a false semblance of Christ set up by religious and institutional rigidity. Dostoevsky's message to everyone, including church leaders is: "Compassion is the most important and, perhaps, the only law of existence for the whole of all mankind."

Consequently, in the world of our underground philosopher ethical ideals do not necessarily lead to the truth. For him, a person who runs away from openly facing the one basic threat—the possibility of non-being—is closer to unbelief than a person who has nothing else to hold onto but his freedom of conscience. Christ gives no other argument when confronted with the Grand Inquisitor in his work *The Brothers Karamazov.* Ethics offers tangible assurances of stability, which Christ rejects as pharisaical.

Having been gifted with the ability to dive deep into the realm of the subconscious, Dostoevsky soon realized how unpredictable human beings can be. His underground man insults his readers, then apologizes and berates himself, which culminates in his becoming aggressive, only to calm down a moment later. And the circle is repeated. He constantly pulls the rug under his own feet, and at the same time he is aware that he is trapped in the labyrinth of his character. He confesses and announces: "Hell, that's me." Such a character—a blend of the humorous and ugly, the pathetic and laughable—is conceivable and bearable only in works of fiction; no one would tolerate him in their home for more than half an hour. Long before Sartre, and more disturbingly than Dante, Dostoevsky described hell in a similar manner, but more accurately: "I maintain that hell is the suffering of being unable to love." Unlike Sartre, this definition of hell does not seek the cause of torture in others but only in oneself, "in my inability to relate to the 'other,' the tragic loneliness of my existential self-containedness, of my 'freedom'," as Yannaras lucidly observed.

Ethical non-determinism

By saying that "to love a person means to see him as God intended him to be," Dostoevsky seems to have set eschatological expectations as the measure of existence in history. By not embellishing the conflicting image of the inhospitable world before him, Dostoevsky composes a grand symphony of life in which paraphony, cacophony and harmony alternate, and moreover coexist, giving us a complex but compelling anthropology. This mixture of good and evil in human nature, susceptibility to sin, the spiritual deviations of his heroes, and cyclic movements from highs to lows and vice versa—all of that is part of his world. The agony and ecstasy of the search for the essence of truth consists of things done right and things done wrong; the beautiful and ugly come across not as aesthetic categories, but rather as hints of what might be hiding behind a face as *les fleurs du mal* (the flowers of evil).

When Dostoevsky rearranges the coordinates of reality in his storytelling (in one story, the snow falls horizontally), he helps the reader to flee from the comfort of the casual narrative. A grave monotony reigns over many devilish forgers of better and brighter futures (Verkhovensky, Stavrogin), whereas those who cherish life, even in bad times and with notable fluctuations in their fortunes, give off a resonance of hope. After all, the latter resonate with a universal frequency, which is why only such people experience a resolving crescendo that comes after a change of heart (*metanoia*) and repentance. Even as a young man Dostoevsky was attracted to Elder Tikhon of Zadonsk, a retired bishop who became the model for all of his elders, precisely because Tikhon was a preacher of repentance, and despite the fact that even in the monastery some distrusted him, accusing him of careless life, and even heresy.

Although a profound psychologist, Dostoevsky does not assess the spiritual rebirth of man in Christ by human criteria alone, nor does he provide a documentary account of such a process. What he does is help us to see how much we have fallen into the trap of self-deception so that we do not dare begin the fight against inherent sinfulness. Whenever we achieve some moral victory, vainglory so muddles our minds that we begin to think that the pride engendered reflects our true self. Alyosha, though, tells his crafty brother: "The ladder's the same. I'm at the bottom step, and you're above, somewhere about the thirteenth. That's how I see it. But it's all the same. Absolutely the same in kind." A sincere God-seeker believes in this humble way and does not conform to the cultural models prescribed by society (or church) by which one seeks to put oneself above the others. Dostoevsky's man lives in flesh and blood and does not hide the pulsation of the living, inner man, thus rejecting the demand of society to recognize in him a "perfect" and "infallible" leader who meets the standards of morality of society.

The purification of love

Although not attempting to diminish the genius of Dostoevsky, Bishop Atanasije also talks about some of his weaknesses: "Some of his characters exhibit elements of pathological love, taking pleasure in inflicting pain on those they claim to love. Dostoevsky himself, I think, appears to have been attracted to this kind of relationship." When asked why he thought that was so, Atanasije replied: "Because, obviously, it was the kind of love that was not completely free from lust and infatuation, not that kind of love at all. Dostoevsky was a deep man with great imagination, but Dostoevsky did not live the life of a saint, of an ascetic." On the other hand, Dostoevsky was honest, and so Atanasije added: "He knew what evil was, what sin was, what passion was, but he should have addressed those issues in his own life; it is not enough to just know about them, one should also strive to put knowledge into action in one's own life. He may have felt that impure love is in fact the source of much torment. That is why love is a struggle; that is why love is a cross." Florovsky observed that the inconsistency and complexity of the Russian soul could be caused by two weaknesses: extreme forbearance and excessive sensitivity. Therefore he wrote that "in the Russian soul there is a treacherous tendency to transformations, a kind of cultural metempsychosis, that Dostoevsky referred to in his speech about Pushkin."

Dostoevsky's name has become synonymous with psychological profundity. The depth and contradictoriness of his heroes have made systematic psychological theories look shallow by comparison. Many theorists (most notably Freud) have tried to claim Dostoevsky as a predecessor. Aware of the relativity of categories of morality in human life, this Russian writer was the first to show that the boundaries between the physical and the psychical in the context of human diversity are not so clear nor unyielding. His sense of evil and his love of freedom made Dostoevsky especially relevant in a century of world wars, mass murders, and totalitarian systems. At least two modern literary genres, the prison camp novel and the dystopian novel (works such as Yevgeny Zamyatin's *We*, Aldous Huxley's *Brave New World*, and George Orwell's *Nineteen Eighty-four*) derive from his writings. His ideas and formal innovations exercised a profound influence on Friedrich Nietzsche, André Gide, Camus, Jean-Paul Sartre, and Mikhail Bulgakov, to name a few.

Dostoevsky did not captivate his readers by the deftly designed, multi-layered structure of his novels alone. Gorky rated him very highly, and even while denouncing him in his speech to the First Congress of Soviet Writers in 1934, he was still capable of comparing Dostoevsky to Shakespeare. That is why he is both a Russian and a European novelist, unforgettable, transformative, and hence universal. As Vasileios Gondikakis (the archimandrite of Iveron Monastery on Mount Athos who learned Russian only to read Fyodor in the original) said, "if you seek what is honorable, what is good, you cannot read Dostoevsky and remain the same. You cannot read him, accept his message and then simply forget it. He becomes yours, and you his. You are entwined with each other in a deep, exalted, wide space, in the open space that belongs to everyone and where everyone fits in."

Going back to the current issue of the man-god (*homo deus*) of Harari, it is clear that Dostoevsky's heroes can restore in us the necessary hope to endure the trials of life. For example, after Raskolnikov (the protagonist of his 1866 novel *Crime and Punishment*) has rationally weighed all conceivable arguments in order to justify his inhumane acts (i.e., he kills an old woman), he nonetheless gets overwhelmed with baffling feelings and impenetrable questions. It is this unpredictability of life that remains a mystery—one that no technology will ever be able to solve because we dwell in a realm beyond algorithms. Dostoevsky's novels illustrate all poles of the antinomy of life, and they can stir us up in this age of transhuman technology. We hope for this to happen while there is still time, so that we can also have heroes worthy of Dostoevsky even in this age.

HAGIA SOPHIA'S UNINTERRUPTED LITURGY

Why did the Russians of San Francisco protest the loudest when the governor of California ordered that singing and chanting in houses of worship be banned under the pretext of the recent pandemic? The answer is simple: ever since they heard the chanting in the church of Hagia Sophia of tenth-century Constantinople, this elaborate form of worship eventually became the most notable feature of Russian church culture.[1] Faith in Christ was transplanted from the City of Constantine (Constantinople) to Russia. As the old Russian *Chronicle* describes, when the envoys of Russian prince Vladimir visited Constantinople, they gained their first experience of the Liturgy by being present at the Divine Liturgy. As Metropolitan John Zizioulas of Pergamon has noted, "The Church in Russia has grown so attached to her initial self-awareness that she herself has developed the solemnity and all the visual and aural splendor of the Divine Liturgy to perfection and attaches far more importance to it than can be observed in other

[1] According to the chronicles, it was the beauty of the liturgy which attracted the attention of Prince Vladimir's emissaries to Constantinople in the 10th century. "We did not know whether we were in Heaven or on earth," they said after attending a celebration at Hagia Sophia.

Orthodox Churches." That is why the Russian bishop told Governor Newsom that the ban on liturgical chanting in places of worship is an infringement on religious freedoms. This raises the question, does the Hagia Sophia as a Christian holy site have any *rights* today?

These days, President Recep Erdogan is simply ignoring the entire civilized and cultural world around him. He pays no attention to the appeals of UNESCO, Moscow, the Vatican, or the White House, just as he did not pay attention to countless appeals of the one who is "clothed in weakness"—Ecumenical Patriarch Bartholomew, who pleaded with him not to continue with the offensive plan to once again make it a mosque. Erdogan has managed to foment inter-religious tension and division through a symbol of unity. And behold the paradox: by turning Hagia Sophia into a mosque, the Turks inadvertently pay respect to her greatness, desiring to experience her unfathomable allure again. No one has been left unaffected by her mysterious grandeur!

On the other hand, the entire world is saddened by the tragic decision of the Turkish authorities to "reconvert" the Hagia Sophia from a museum to a mosque. Many have justly protested the decision of the civil courts in Turkey and have tried to intervene in order to change this decision. They petitioned that Saint Sophia should remain a museum, precisely because they respect her beginnings and subsequent history. The Russian Patriarch said that this threat against

***The Hagia Sophia*,**
acrylic on canvas, 2020, by Bishop Maxim

The Hagia Sophia is a marvelous building that transcends time and still impacts Christianity's history. Its importance came to light recently with the decision to convert it into a mosque. This acrylic painting depicts the exterior of the Hagia Sophia ("Holy Wisdom," Sancta Sophia, Ayasofya) with the sea walls of Constantinople. It seems that Justinian's dream of the Eastern Roman Empire's sea power was imprinted here. The ellipticity of the dome seems to be the origin and crowning of the peculiar light of the Hagia Sophia.

Hagia Sophia is a threat to all of Christian civilization. This is not a coincidence, for "The Russians would never have become Christians, had it not been for the Hagia Sophia," said St. Nicholai of Zhicha on January 12, 1920, in the Cathedral of St. Paul in London. Is it time for Byzantium and Russia to meet again now that both are wounded? What should, however, concern us more than the conversion of the church into a mosque is that the voices of Christians of the 21st century have become so inaudible. The powerful message of the Resurrection does not resonate in the world today, and many of us Christians share the blame for the current fiasco.

This is not the first time that the lament of the Christian people has been heard. The late medieval elegy, *Poem of Hagia Sophia*, composed after the fall of Constantinople, has become relevant again.

'God signifies, the earth signifies, the heavens signify,
And so too does Hagia Sophia, the great monastery
With its four hundred semantrons and its sixty-two
  bells,
Every bell and priest, every priest and deacon.
The emperor recites the psalmody on the left, the
  patriarch recites
it on the right,
And the columns are shaken by the great psalmody.
Let the emperor recite the cherubic hymn and let him
  come out.
Their shout comes from heaven and from the mouth of
  an archangel:

"Stop reciting the cherubicon and bring down the holy [vessels].
Let the bishops take the sacred vessels, and may you extinguish
your candles,
Because it is the will of God that the City should fall to the Turks
Transmit my word to France to send three ships,
One to take the cross and the other to take the gospel book,
The third, the best, to take our holy altar
Lest [the Turks] take it as booty and make us convert to Islam."
The Despoina [Theotokos] was troubled and the icons wept, (saying):
"Be silent, lady Despoina, and do not weep too much,
It shall again be yours with the passing of years, with the passing of Time.'"

The following words of St. Nicholai of Zhicha are likewise stirring: "The Hagia Sophia is the most faithful and magnificent exposition of Christian doctrine and Christian duty—she represents the beginning and the end of the world; this is her mystical significance." And in the spirit of those words, we are called to rise above the daily, biased and overly politicized discussions about this topic. While one hegemon signs a decree on changing the status of the Hagia Sophia, the result of which is its conversion into a functioning mosque, Christians can find comfort and hope again by learning about her secrets and legends, and by listening to her voice. Today maybe more than ever before.

What can we, ordinary people, learn from this? What do we really know about the Hagia Sophia? Certainly, we will never remain indifferent to the incomprehensible splendor of this Mother Church. More than two decades ago, Charalambos Stathakis wrote the book *The Hagia Sophia—The Mystical Light of the Great Church and Its Architectural Dress*. By reading his descriptions of the most minute details, the reader gains a vision of the Great Church, not just as a glorious building, but as a living entity with personal characteristics. Stathakis, an outstanding doctor and philanthropist, takes your hand and leads you to a secret tunnel in the underground world of Constantinople that opens to the vestibule of Hagia Sophia. This helps you to understand, as much as you can, this Church that appears unassuming in the experience she conveys, but not in her structure and structural solutions. She *reveals* herself to us gradually, mystagogically. The author's originality in the interpretation of architecture and space lies in placing the idea of *light* as the hermeneutic key to understanding her power. The point of the author can be summarized as follows: "This place and type of life is the Hagia Sophia, the Holy Wisdom of God, because the Word of God, the Second person of the Holy Trinity, the Son, the Strength and Wisdom of the Father, sanctifies the building and lives in it as an Image of Light."

I would like to make one perhaps "mistaken" but, I hope, proactive suggestion: Why could Hagia Sophia not belong to both—and therefore to *all*? Could the neo-Ottoman Erdogan—who, unfortunately, will *not listen* to the appeals from all over the world for Hagia Sophia to remain a museum—amend his decree with a clause allowing Christians to serve the Liturgy on Sundays or Holidays, if not in the central, then in one of her side naves? And if not there, then maybe in the upper south gallery where the Ecumenical Councils were held and where the famous Deisis mosaic is located (the art of the Palaeologi—the last but timeless accord of the Byzantine great symphony)? Whether this is some kind of Solomonic solution or not, I do not know. Syncretism aside, I know that in that way Hagia Sophia would again embrace all the inhabitants of the city with her arms. Can Erdogan—and modern Turkey—achieve such a degree of humanity?

The battle for the Hagia Sophia has never ceased nor is it hopeless. For, if her devastating transformation into a mosque means our loss, then perhaps she is not so powerful after all. On the other hand, it may be that the purpose of Hagia Sophia is not to be owned, but to *have* all of us, without exception, as her *own*.

In all this, the unfathomable Hagia Sophia remains silent and unperturbed. She just keeps comforting us, forgiving us, and calling us to repentance. Perhaps it would not be bad for us Christians today to listen to the quiet voice of Hagia Sophia again. Let us look at her humbleness in order to see ourselves better, because she is "the eye of the universe," as she was called by St. Photius the Great on March 25, 862. Why not consider that along with the material loss we are also offered something purer and more reconcilable—that is, the Hypostatic Wisdom of God. After all, the temples that reference Sophia (Wisdom) in Byzantium always have *Christ* as their central theme, and not some divine attribute or a female principle—as Fr. George Florovsky showed.

The logic of Saint Sophia is the logic of the One who sacrifices Himself in order to save what is His—that is, everyone, even those who hate Him, spit on Him and crucify Him. In the words of a wise man from Mount Athos: "That is the only logic—the reversal of our paralogical logic. It is the Divine reconciliation in Christ, who is Love." Perhaps on her cross-bearing road, Hagia Sophia will continue to raise the dead with her uninterrupted Liturgy.

Beethoven,
acrylic on canvas, 2021, Bishop Maxim

This is a surprising "Beethoven." Hair flies from the urge of inspiration. The eyes—the strongest point of the painting—are in ecstasy. The red cowl also participates in ecstasy. A book, a keyboard, and a clock—everything floats, terrified by the invisible waves of fate. The presence of a floating clock is important, indicating the connection between the mystery of time and the mystery of music. Beethoven's wide gaze and the semicircular keyboard indicate the comprehensiveness, enormous energy, and great momentum which envelops the drama of existence, from the germ of the Big Bang to the future mystery of the Eschaton.

LIST OF ILLUSTRATIONS

INDEX

ABOUT THE AUTHOR

Bishop Maxim (Vasiljević) of Los Angeles and Western America earned his doctorate from the University of Athens in the field of dogmatics and patristics in 1999, and was tonsured at the Monastery of Tvrdoš in Bosnia and Herzegovina. He entertained a one-year post-doctoral course on Byzantine History and Theology at the Sorbonne in Paris from 2003–4. At the same time, as a visiting professor at the French Academy of Fine Arts (Beaux-arts) in Paris, he engaged in the theory and practice of painting. As a painter he had multiple exhibits in Europe and the USA. In addition to his tenure at the School of Orthodox Theology of the University of Belgrade, Bishop Maxim has served as a member of the faculty of the University of East Sarajevo (1998–2006) and is currently teaching at Holy Cross Greek Orthodox School of Theology. He has taught numerous courses on the writings of the Church Fathers and published widely in the field of patristics, hagiography, Church history, and iconography. In 2006, he was elected bishop of the Western American Diocese of the Serbian Orthodox Church. Besides numerous books and scholarly articles, his bibliography includes: *History, Truth, Holiness* (Los Angeles, Sebastian Press: 2011), *Diary of the Council* (Los Angeles-Crete 2016), *Holiness: Divine and Human* (Belgrade: 2010, in Serbian), *Theology as a Surprise* (New York, St. Vladimir Seminary Press: 2018), *Seeing the Invisible* (Belgrade: 2020, in Serbian), *The Portraits of Dostoevsky's Heroes* (Belgrade: 2022, in Serbian), and *Accomplishing the Future in Advance* (Brepols 2023 – forthcoming).

HERE ENDS THE BOOK, "WONDER AS THE BEGINNING OF FAITH" BY MAXIM VASILJEVIC, FOREWORDED BY CHRISTOS YANNARAS, AND TRANSLATED FROM SERBIAN BY TEODORA GITA SIMIC. THIS EDITION IS LIMITED TO 1000 COPIES, PRINTED AT THE INTERKLIMA-GRAFIKA PRESS IN VRNJCI, SERBIA, REALIZED BY HOLY CROSS ORTHODOX PRESS IN BROOKLINE, MASSACHUSETTS, AND FINISHED ON THE 10TH DAY OF MAY IN THE YEAR OF THE LORD 2022.

HOLY CROSS
ORTHODOX PRESS